Speaking of Religion . . .

Speaking of Religion . . .

Approaching the Academic Study of Religion with Compassion, Conviction, and Civility

ROY HAMMERLING

CASCADE *Books* • Eugene, Oregon

SPEAKING OF RELIGION . . .
Approaching the Academic Study of Religion with Compassion, Conviction, and Civility

Copyright © 2022 Roy Hammerling. All rights reserved. Except for brief quotations in critical publications or reviews, no part of this book may be reproduced in any manner without prior written permission from the publisher. Write: Permissions, Wipf and Stock Publishers, 199 W. 8th Ave., Suite 3, Eugene, OR 97401.

Cascade Books
An Imprint of Wipf and Stock Publishers
199 W. 8th Ave., Suite 3
Eugene, OR 97401

www.wipfandstock.com

PAPERBACK ISBN: 978-1-6667-3086-9
HARDCOVER ISBN: 978-1-6667-2287-1
EBOOK ISBN: 978-1-6667-2288-8

Cataloguing-in-Publication data:

Names: Hammerling, Roy [author].

Title: Speaking of religion . . . : approaching the academic study of religion with compassion, conviction, and civility / Roy Hammerling.

Description: Eugene, OR: Cascade Books, 2022 | Includes bibliographical references and index.

Identifiers: ISBN 978-1-6667-3086-9 (paperback) | ISBN 978-1-6667-2287-1 (hardcover) | ISBN 978-1-6667-2288-8 (ebook)

Subjects: LCSH: Religion—Study and teaching | Religions—Relations | Religious studies | Theology—Study and teaching | Dialogue—Religious aspects | Religion—Methodology

Classification: BL41 H36 2022 (paperback) | BL41 (ebook)

02/24/22

This book is dedicated to Rev. Sarah Rohde
and to all my former students who wrestled with this text in class.
Thank you for being my teachers.
I also dedicate it to past students who were crazy enough to go off to
graduate school and become teachers themselves: amazingly you are
too many to name here, but you know who you are—thank you for
your courage and willingness to guide the next generation.
Lastly, I dedicate this to my former teachers, especially Mrs. Knoor,
Lee Boyk, Ken Scherr, Kenneth Christopherson, Ralph Gehrke, Ralph
Quere, Dan Sheerin, and John Van Engen, who in their love of the
journey of learning helped their students to fly
beyond weighty earthbound simpleminded beliefs
to the stars of the mysterious universe
of the compassionate, convicted, and civil conversation.

In Memory
of
William Alan Ekberg
(May 27, 1923 to June 14, 2016)

In Memory
of
Dr. Shawn Carruth, O.S.B.
(June 18, 1942 to March 26, 2020)
Prioress of Mount St. Benedict Crookston, Minnesota
Master Educator Concordia College, Moorhead, Minnesota

She listened closely
to the master's instructions
and attended to them
with the ear of her heart;
she continually reminded us
to remember our humanity;
and sadly, she hastened
to the heavenly homeland
before us.

Contents

Acknowledgements | ix

   Introduction: An Invitation to a Risky Endeavor | 1

1 The Academic Study of Religion: What Is Religion Anyway? | 6

2 Speaking of Religion: A Disorienting Experience | 33

3 First Encounters with the Academic Study of Religion: Case Studies | 44

4 A Safe Space: Getting into the Hallway | 67

5 Healthy Dialogue: The Uncommon Decency of Compassionate Convicted Civility | 77

6 Creating Conscience: Discovering Self | 92

   Conclusion: Living the Questions | 114

Bibliography | 119

Index | 123

Acknowledgements

"We can easily forgive a child
who is afraid of the dark.
The real tragedy of life is when adults
are afraid of the light."

—Attributed to Plato (d. circa 347 BCE)
Cf. *The Republic* Book 7

This work is deeply indebted to roughly five hundred students who have read this text with me over the past decade. I have adapted the work according to their suggestions. While I cannot acknowledge them in the way they deserve, I thank them most heartily for their advice and wisdom. I only hope these pages do justice to what they've taught me. I would like to especially acknowledge Rev. Sarah Rohde for her strong encouragement to write this book in the first place. Thank you for your wise counsel, friendship, and important contribution to this work. Likewise, my sincere appreciation goes out to Hannah Papenfuss, Luke Papenfuss, Emma Rifai, and Nadia Toumeh for adding their voices and insights to chapter 3. I'm grateful to Kenny David, Riley Erlandson, Liesl Francisco, Ingrid Jacobson, Mallory Rabehl, Sammy Strootman, William Southworth, and Zach Strickland, the "CSL Club," the relentless lovers of learning, who offered criticism and inspiration on the final draft of this project. All of the above have been fellow pilgrims on the path; thank you for making the journey a joy.

I would be remiss not to acknowledge the invaluable scholarly feedback of selfless colleagues who read and showed me how to improve the

Acknowledgements

work. Most notably I'd like to thank Michelle Lelwica, who besides her abiding friendship, has offered me acute observations and support in the process of writing. Thank you, Jacqueline Bussie for giving me keen insights and showing a special enthusiasm for this endeavor. I am grateful to David Creech, Stewart Herman, Michael Johnson, Hilda Koster, Anne Mocko, Jan Pranger, Ernie Simmons, and Elna Solvang, the members of the Concordia College Religion Department: you all have given me precious advice and comfort over the years. I am also beholden to my tireless administrative assistants Mary Thornton, Elizabeth Cronin, Hannah Balko, and Mark Melby: I offer you a most heartfelt *thank you*. A particular appreciation goes out to Stephanie Ahlfeldt and Darlene Ross who provided me with Sabbatical Scholarship Funds to defray some of the costs of this work.

In the past, I have been fortunate to have worked with Machien Justin Luoi and Gat-kier Machar and many others of PACODES (Panyijiar Community Development Services), a not-for-profit organization, which benefits the Lost Boys, Lost Girls, and families of South Sudan, the Panyijiar region, by providing education to an area of the world with a 98 percent illiteracy rate. The inspirational work of this organization and especially the generous hearts of Machien and Gat-kier, their families, the Lost Boys and Girls, and the talented board of directors Joan Kopperud, Ron Twedt, Richard Chapman, Mike Bath, and Bethmarie Gooding is a never-failing source of inspiration to me.

My thanks also belongs to the staff at Cascade Books, especially Rev. Dr. Robin Parry and his fine team. Your help made this book better in every way.

Finally, it gives me great joy to thank my family. Thanks to my son, Jeremiah and his wife Rita Baghdadi, who have provided me with insight into the nature of the human condition through their art of film. Thanks to my daughter, Rachel and her husband Calvin Miller, who have shown me how a good thoughtful liberal arts education, which includes the study of religion, can truly make a difference in the world of nursing. I am overwhelmed by the love of their children Olin, Wells, and Brooks, who remind me every day about what really matters in life. I likewise thank our youngest, Josh, and his wife Dr. Jessie Hammerling, for their keen mindful love of life: thanks Josh for commenting on early drafts of this work. In the end, however, my deepest gratitude belongs to Peggy, who is the one without whom the world would not turn for me. Your compassionate honesty and loving support are the only way any work I have ever done has been accomplished.

Introduction

An Invitation to a Risky Endeavor

"Not all those who wander are lost."

—J. R. R. Tolkien (d. 1973), *The Lord of the Rings*

This book is an invitation to a risky endeavor: an enticement to compassionate, convicted, and civil conversations about religion. It is for anyone interested in learning how to explore a caring critical examination of the meaning of life with others. For some, their sense of purpose is rooted in religious beliefs and for others it is in philosophically oriented worldviews that are as far away from religion as they can get. Either way, this work is for whoever desires to study the deep mysteries of life with friends, in a classroom, in study groups, or across a table in a coffee shop with strangers.

Beware: the enterprise of the academic study of religion (ASR) hazards a willingness to venture into the unknown. The ASR rushes in with a bold reckless abandon to pursue answers to the most troubling issues of human existence. It demands that we confront and not simply ignore our daily experiences of death, evil, suffering, love, joy, and what we think about God. It moves hearts and minds to wonder concerning the great marvels of everyday living. It challenges us to assess and reassess our ways of understanding the world and requires that we scrutinize both our hot heads and cold hearts with cool reason and warm compassionate consciences amid clear critical analysis. And it does so with people who have views that may seem to be light years away from our beliefs.

Speaking of Religion...

First and foremost, the risk primarily is to *us*. We often would rather walk with easy answers and not complicate our lives too much: the smooth road more traveled in other words. Still, for many of us such simple paths will not do. Augustine of Hippo 1,500 years ago suggested that we must first believe if we can ever to seek understanding.[1] The ASR beckons us down a hard way, along a road that searches out our consciences and firmly held convictions about how the world works so we may grasp what we believe. Then we will be free to understand. However, in order to do this, we must chance the disorientation and the frustration of meandering down various ways that are not always obvious or well-defined with companions that we may not have chosen. There is always hope that the wandering path will lead to at least a small measure of insight and wisdom. As J. R. R. Tolkien once noted, "Not all who wander are lost."[2]

The ASR stimulates compassionate exchanges between worlds: the world of our ideals and reality; our world and the worlds of others. It strives for compassionate, convicted, and civil dialogue. Without honest humility on our parts, however, this will never happen. When done well and properly, speaking about religion can prick consciences, embolden imaginations, and motivate us to act with kindness towards others, ourselves, and the world.

In the public sphere today, talk on the topic of religion often divides more than it unites. We currently live in a climate of religious, cultural, and political turmoil. The ASR, however, has as one of its loftiest goals to discover a way through the morass. This cannot be done unless we put the shoulders of our hearts and minds to grindstones. Strenuous effort, however, is not enough in and of itself. The ASR endeavors to create a better world by promoting interfaith dialogue and affectionate collaboration that is rooted in conscience and trustworthy actions. The task may seem to some to be doomed from the start, but that is not what I have found. Sincere open dialogue can transform the lives of those who dare to venture into the breach between "us" and "them." Surely it is a perilous business, but the ASR can provide a safe space amid the dangerous divisions of everyday intolerance where compassionate, convicted, and civil conversations can happen.

Toward the turn of the millennium, early on in my now nearly thirty-year career as an instructor of religion classes at Concordia College in Moorhead, Minnesota, students began to struggle more and more with

---

1. Augustine, *In Evangelium Ioannis Tractatus Centum Viginti Quator* 29:6.
2. Tolkien, *The Fellowship of the Ring*, 186.

Introduction

the basic distinction between being religious—or being dedicated to an ideological worldview—and the study of religion as an academic discipline. After 9/11, Americans, as well as many around the globe, allowed religious and political polarization free reign. Some students in my classes began to have difficulty engaging in speaking about religion in a compassionate manner because their own feelings about their firmly held personal convictions got in the way. Somehow, we had arrived at a place where it was not only fashionable, but crucial for some to cling to hard prejudices about others, who did not share their beliefs. Conversations became tense, civility was hard to come by, and compassion was buried under the mudslide of needing to be right.

Christian Smith, a sociology of religion professor at the University of Notre Dame, suggests that the rise of the Christian religious right, during the latter part of the twentieth century, strongly contributed to our present-day anxiety over speaking about religion. The "moral majority" made a convincing case for many that religion could not be divorced from political ideology and policy. They advocated for a blending of faith and politics, suggesting that politicians and laws both needed to be more "Christian"—by which they meant a type of Christianity that they labeled as Evangelical or conservative. As a result, the self-styled "moral majority" began to promote the Republican Party and candidates from the pulpit and lecterns. This made Christians of a more liberal bent, who were more dedicated to a separation of church and state, uncomfortable and so they in-turn sought to build up barricades against such thinking. People outside of Christian circles also joined one side or other based upon their political values, which flowed out of their own religious or philosophical convictions. Lines were drawn in the cultural sand; demonization of the other side became more pronounced; cooperation in politics between parties began to break down; victory came to mean disagreeing without compromise and winning was valued over civil discourse. The common good became a casualty of self-righteous divisions. This conflict naturally spilled over into a wider public arena, especially classrooms where speaking about religion was regularly engaged in.[3]

On a continuum, after 9/11, my students either became more defensive about speaking about religion or they retreated into timidity as they encountered opinions that were at odds with their own. Some who called themselves Evangelical Christians at times believed that the function of

---

3. Smith, *Divided by Faith*.

religion classes was to indoctrinate their classmates. If others, or I as the instructor, did not readily agree with a comment they made, they at times felt a need, and even a duty, to convert us to what they considered their obviously superior religious ideals. One student even cheerfully shared with me in my office one day that he had gone to a conservative Christian summer Bible camp in which counselors "trained" him on how to argue against teachers, like me, who sought open, authentic dialogue about religion in a neutral setting, where differences were celebrated. He explicitly told me that his goal was not only to change the minds of others, but to disrupt conversations about religious matters that did not go along with what he called in air quotes, "The capital 'T' Truth." Classes with these students at times woefully devolved into heated debates around issues like the literal interpretation of the Bible (especially Genesis and the creation story), abortion, climate change, gender, and race issues, and so forth.

Others, who had very little religious upbringing, but still identified with a religious tradition nominally, felt out of place: as a result, some became timid in conversation. Agnostics and atheists at times worried that their philosophical convictions would not be taken seriously and dreaded that they would be asked to abandon their consciences in favor of the religious worldview of the instructor, institution, other students, or the author they might be reading. Their responses to speaking about religion and difference depended a lot on their personality.

Of course, most students who undertake the ASR fit somewhere between extremes. All, however, come to the ASR with some fear and trembling. Likewise, people who talk about religion in a public, and even in family settings of late, have found that landmines abound. Stepping on certain topics that have political ramifications can easily lead to a blow up. As the years wore on, it took me longer and longer to help students move to a place where they actually felt safe enough to listen to their classmates and speak to them with convicted civility, as Martin Marty has called it.[4]

Marty helpfully recognized as early as the 1960s that there is often a "tragic breach" that exists between those who take the time to study religion and workaday believers outside of academic settings in churches, synagogues, mosques, and temples.[5] The fissure, I believe, has become more menacing. Compassionate conversations recently have been drowned out worldwide with shouts from the fringes calling for no compromise.

4. Marty, *By Way of Response*, 8.
5. Thielicke, *A Little Exercise for Young Theologians*, xii.

Introduction

Standing one's ground and never crossing the aisle of religious and political difference is perceived as a sign of strength, even if it means grinding the process of helping people to a halt. A willingness to listen and have open and frank discussions about things that matter are regularly ridiculed. Many have simply settled for whispered exchanges with those who know their secret partisan passwords: this specifically has become worse with the rise of social media, where people have learned to retreat into narrow-minded chatrooms. Emotionally laden jargon and flippant labels are thrown like tar upon opponents in order to minimize similarities, exaggerate differences, and obliterate common ground. Martin Marty has pointedly noted that people with the deepest convictions all too often lack civility, while the people who are civil, regularly don't want to get involved and therefore appear unconvicted.[6]

Clearly in this environment learning to speak compassionately, in a convicted manner, and with civility about religion is needed more than ever. I hope that this book will be useful in providing a starting place where people may learn compassionate, convicted, and civil dialogue. Similarly, Richard Mouw, the former president of the conservative Christian Fuller Theological Seminary, has advocated for what he calls "uncommon decency."[7] Allow me, therefore, to offer this book as an invitation into a safe space, where we can learn more about ourselves even as we engage others with fruitful and compassionate dialogue about matters that concern us all.

In the movie *Shadowlands* about the life of C. S. Lewis, a character says, "We read to know that we are not alone." Hopefully reading this book will reveal that it is a basic quality of being human to reach for answers to the greatest questions of our existence: "Does God exist?" "If not, why not?" And if so, "Who is God?" "Or are there many gods?" "Why do we suffer?" "What is evil?" "What happens when we die?" "How do we lead a virtuous life?" "How do I love my enemy?" When we seek answers together, despite our differences, we can begin to understand ourselves and others in a way that can create caring connections that move us to make our communities and our world a kinder place that values the common good of all people. The ASR in the end risks nothing less than hoping to discover the meaning of life for ourselves and others, so we may live compassionate, convicted, and civil lives.

---

6. Marty, *Education, Religion and the Common Good*, 100.
7. Mouw, *Uncommon Decency*.

1

The Academic Study of Religion
What Is Religion Anyway?

"I will not consider something to be good just because it is new or to be bad because it is old."

—Helmut Thielicke (d. 1986) *Notes from a Wayfarer.*

"*Fides quaerens intellectum*"
"I have faith seeking understanding."

—Anselm (d. 1109), *Proslogium*

We all know what religion is, but actually defining it can be a challenge. Etymological studies of the word "religion" suggest a few possible origins. Cicero (d. 43 BCE), the Roman philosopher and statesman, argued that the word religion comes from the Latin *relegere*, which he breaks down this way: *re* means "again" and *legere* "to read"—together they mean something like "to thoroughly consider." *Religio* for Cicero refers to the beliefs that we hold to be true, because we have examined troubling life questions and have come to some semblance of an answer about them. Such considerations move us to engage in specific ritual observances, to adopt specific teachings, to act according to specific morals, and to define virtue in a particular way.[1]

Other scholars point to Augustine of Hippo (d. 420 CE), one of the most influential Christian theologians in the early church, who suggested that the word goes back to the Latin *religare*, where *ligare* means "to bind." Some point out that *ligare* is connected to our modern English word "ligament."[2] Augustine's autobiography, *Confessions*, explores Augustine's encounters with evil, sin, suffering, vice, virtue, conscience, love, grace, and God. Augustine, by retracing his steps through his memory from his infancy onward, concluded that his heart was always tied to what he believed he loved the most. "My weight is my love,"[3] he notably observed. If he loved wealth, fame, or power then he was weighted down by striving after them. Eventually he sought after a more lasting peace, which for him was only found when he returned to his Creator, whom he called Beauty, ancient and new. When he set aside his earthly desires, and bound himself eternal things, such as love, Augustine discovered not only what he believed but how to act. His faith moved him to seek understanding by thinking critically, acting lovingly, and pursuing wisdom. He argued that whatever we bind our bodies, hearts, minds, and spirits to is our religion and God. The entire *Confessions* is Augustine's quest for rest, to untie himself from a restless life and to bind himself to that which gives rest. Or as he famously observed, "Our hearts are restless, until they rest in You, O God."[4]

For Cicero and Augustine, religion was not simply a mental ascent to truth, but the hope of attaining a peace that poured forth in faithful lives that had both meaning and purpose. But such answers are not always satisfactory to those who want to speak about religion. William James the famous philosopher and early psychologist, about a century ago, helpfully pointed out the problem of focusing too narrowly on singular definitions of religion:

> The very fact that [definitions of religion] are so many and so different from one another that this is enough to prove that the word "religion" cannot stand for any single principle or essence, but is

---

1. Bragova, "Cicero on the Gods and Roman Religion," 303–13; see also Lewis, *An Elementary Latin Dictionary*.

2. *The Online Etymological Dictionary*, "religion."

3. Augustine, *Confessions* 13.9.10.

4. Besides Augustine's *Confessions* and his *City of God*, 10.3 see Lactantius *Divinae Institutiones* IV.28.

rather a collective name.... Let us not fall immediately into a one-sided view of our subject but let us rather admit freely at the outset that we may very likely not find one essence, but many characters which may alternately be equally important to religion.[5]

With James's caution in mind, I personally, have found when speaking about religion that it is productive to explore the ideas of Friedrich von Hügel (d. 1925), a Roman Catholic scholar of religion, when attempting to think analytically about religion. Hügel's definition has many sides to it, which are firmly rooted within his historical context. As a result, it requires some context and reinterpretation for a modern audience.

During Hügel's day, there were at least three major points of conflict that developed between religion and science, the two most honored ways of knowing. Today the debate has lost little of the initial vigor. As the major tensions between religion and science developed, Hügel took the unusual stand that he did not believe that religion and science needed to be in contention with each other, but rather should be seen as complimentary ways of understanding the mysteries of the universe. To fully grasp the significance of his ideas, let us first look closely at the major points of contention.

The first point of disagreement developed when *The Origin of the Species* was published in 1859 by Charles Darwin (d. 1892). At the time, some religious scholars, like the Rev. Charles Kingsley (d. 1875)—a priest in the Anglican Church, English university professor, novelist, and a friend of Darwin, took the position that science, and especially Darwin's theories, revealed how God had created a wonderful world in which creatures had the ability of "self-development into other needful forms." Kingsley believed that God's work of creation was not finished but was ongoing in creatures by means of the process of evolution.[6] Religion and science, Kingsley noted, were compatible in that both were needed to understand the world properly. Should people only rely on one method, their understanding of the world would be incomplete. Others disagreed.

Within a year of the publication of the *Origin of the Species*, the "1860 Oxford Evolution Debate" took place. Modern readers are often surprised to learn that Darwin himself had been baptized as an Anglican, later attended the Unitarian church, and even studied to be an Anglican pastor at one point. At the "1860 Oxford Evolution Debate," however, Darwin and Kingsley's views were strongly opposed by many religious leaders who

---

5. James, *Varieties of Religious Experience*, 27.
6. See Kingsley's closing remarks in Darwin, *On the Origins of the Species*, 481.

viewed some scientific conclusions about the origins of humanity as not only preposterous, but in opposition to religious ways of understanding the origins of the universe. Perhaps the most famous aspect of the Oxford debate was what is now considered a legendary exchange between an Anglican Bishop, Samuel Wilberforce (d. 1873), and Thomas Henry Huxley, an English biologist and anthropologist, also known as "Darwin's bulldog," because he defended evolutionary theory. Supposedly Wilberforce asked Huxley, whether he was descended from apes on his grandmother or grandfather's side of the family. Huxley, so the legend goes, allegedly responded that he would rather be descended from apes than anyone who did not take scientific investigation seriously.[7]

Wilberforce and others believed that Darwin's observations about evolution amounted to a secular, and ultimately unholy, explanation of how life originated on earth. They, therefore, saw evolutionary scientific evidence as a threat to what they considered to be God's revealed truth in biblical texts, especially the creation story of Genesis and the idea that God was the Creator of all that exists.

It is helpful to point out that many during the mid-nineteenth century were not biblical literalists, but the conviction gained popularity in response to the rise of scientific advancements. Biblical literalism became an important defensive argument against science for some. The view suggested that the Bible was literally true, and science was false when it contradicted that truth.[8] On the other end of the debate, a group of scientists dismissed religion outright as being nothing more than silly superstitious beliefs completely devoid of reason. Even today, a conflict rages, especially dealing with primary and secondary school curriculums, between those who advocate for creationism, intelligent design, or modern biblical literalism over and against scientific views, especially evolution.[9]

If Darwin's theories weren't bad enough for some, along came a second threat in Sigmund Freud (d. 1939), a scientist who studied neurology and was foundational in developing psychoanalysis. Raised in a devout Jewish household, Freud later became an ardent atheist. In his book *The Future of an Illusion* (1927), he suggested that religion was handed down to

---

7. *Oxford Chronicle*, 7 July 1850. See also Ungureanu, "A Yankee at Oxford."

8. For more see Armstrong, *The Bible: The Biography*.

9. There are numerous books that have been written recently on the topic of Creationism vs. Evolution. A quick search will indicate that both sides are working hard to make their case.

the present day by their ancestors, who taught ideas that often were simply accepted without reasoned thought. Instead, Freud suggested that if people actually looked at their religious beliefs closely, they would see that they were nothing more than "wish fulfillments" of their oldest and strongest human desires. Discussing why people still rely on religion, Freud concluded, "The gods retain the threefold task: they must exorcise the terrors of nature, they must reconcile [people] to the cruelty of Fate, particularly as it is shown in death, and they must compensate them for the sufferings and privations which a civilized life in common has imposed on them."[10] Ultimately, religion was a societal neurosis that needed to be abandoned, said Freud, in favor of more scientific explanations about the human psyche. Psychoanalysis became a widely accepted legitimate scientific pursuit, largely because of its ability to help people. Today the discipline has moved away from some its founder's views, but some religious people still remain very hesitant concerning this science because of Freud's atheism.

Karl Marx (d. 1883), the political theorist, economist, philosopher, historian, and noted atheist, was born into an ethnic, but not religious Jewish household. Though never very devout, his father did convert to Protestantism. Marx wrote the *Communist Manifesto* in 1848 and he is regularly given credit as being one of the originators of social science. Marx, for some, rounded out the unholy trinity of suspect authors who relied on science and denigrated religion. Marx's promotion of the idea of communism, as an alternative to western capitalism, did not help matters. With regard to religion Marx noted, "Religion is the sigh of the oppressed creature, the heart of a heartless world, and the soul of a soulless conditions. It is the opium of the people."[11]

Many religious people of his day perceived of Marx's ideas as being incompatible with religion and a serious threat to their way of life. With the rise of the Soviet Union's brand of atheistic communism, people in the West feared its attack on their cultural values and even worried about a militaristic threat. Media and churches in the USA referred to Russian communism as "godless" and lifted up America as a "Christian Nation." The belief that God would fulfill human destiny by converting the world to Christianity by means of the influence of the USA was perpetuated. Nikita Khrushchev representing the opposite view said, "History is on our side. We will bury you." The Cold War heated up. Today in the USA, if one party wants to

10. Freud, *Future of an Illusion*, 19.
11. Karl Marx, "A Contribution to the Critique of Hegel's Philosophy of Right."

denigrate those on the other end of the political spectrum, they label them with terms like Nazi, communist, or socialist seeking to marginalize them even further by digging up old tried and true methods of stirring up fear, hate, and violence.

At about the same time as Darwin, Freud, and Marx, the French philosopher Auguste Comte (d. 1857) in his *The Course of Positive Philosophy* (1842) put forth the law of three stages of society. Comte argued societies in the earliest stage of human development, which he called the theological stage, were primitive and believed that spirits inhabited inanimate objects. Our ancestors attributed godly qualities to these spirits and polytheism developed. Over time, Comte believed that there was a move away from polytheism to more monotheistic beliefs. Comte called this the metaphysical stage, when a more abstract and less anthropomorphic view of God emerged: God was now perceived of as a force that controlled the universe. Comte finally suggested that societies would naturally and inevitably develop into intellectual, positive, or scientifically oriented communities in what he deemed the positivity stage. In the end, science would ultimately supplant religion. For Comte, this was inevitable and a good development, because religions were primitive, and science was the only sensible way of seeking truth.

Many have echoed Comte's convictions. Anthony F. C. Wallace (d. 2015), the eminent anthropologist, in his *Religion: An Anthropological View* expected in 1966 that religion would soon die out in the wake of scientific advances, which were now able to understand the farthest corners of the cosmos.[12] Scientists like Richard Dawkins (b. 1941), Sam Harris (b. 1967), Colin Blakemore (b. 1944), Stephen Hawking (d. 2018), and others have suggested that religion hinders productive societies: in fact, religion is detrimental to such goals. And yet, religion today not only persists, but it also thrives. Why?

Peter Harrison,[13] in his article "Why Religion Is Not Going Away and Science Will Not Destroy It," wonders why secularist views about the demise of religion have not come to pass. He suggests a variety of reasons. He reminds his reader that there have been some remarkable historical experiments in the past that have sought to remove or minimize religion's influence in specific countries. He points to two very different secular revolutions as

---

12. Wallace, *Religion*.

13. Harrison is the director of the Institute for Advanced Studies in the Humanities at the University of Queensland, Australia.

examples: the twentieth-century communist Russian revolution and Mustafa Kemal Atatürk's new Turkish republic, founded in the 1920s. Both gave science a favored place in education and political programs, but neither was able to create a religion-free, purely scientific-centered society. Indeed, religious adherents in both countries today have not only survived but have become entrenched and widespread. Russian Orthodoxy never completely disappeared and with the fall of communism rebounded dramatically. In recent years, various Muslim groups have noticeably grown in influence throughout Turkey, especially conservatives in the political arena.

Harrison contends, "If anything, it is science that is subject to increasing threats to its authority and social legitimacy," rather than the other way around. Harrison provides a few illustrations. While a keystone of science is Darwin's theory of evolution, many fundamentalist groups today have successfully promoted and enshrined their alternative views of creationism or intelligent design in some schools. Harrison concludes, "Given this, science needs all the friends it can get. Its advocates would be well advised to stop fabricating an enemy out of religion or insisting that the only path to a secure future lies in a marriage of science and secularism."[14]

Carl Sagan (d. 1996), the astrophysicist, astrobiologist, and popularizer of science, also worried that people who urge a scientific worldview to the exclusion of religion are not thinking practically. He says that the skeptical movement, as he calls it, is doing more harm than good. Discussing this issue, he wrote, "The chief deficiency I see in the skeptical movement is its polarization: Us vs. Them—the sense that we have a monopoly on truth; that those other people who believe in all these stupid doctrines are morons; that if you're sensible, you'll listen to us; and if not, to hell with you. This is nonconstructive. It does not get our message across. It condemns us to permanent minority status."[15] Both Harrison and Sagan believed that a world in which religion and science work together is a much better model and way forward into the future.

Now, let us return to Friedrich von Hügel, who suggested, as the debate was heating up at the beginning of the twentieth century, that if truth is truth, then religion and science do not need to be in conflict with each other. Rather, they desperately need to find ways in which both can be used

---

14. Harrison, "Why Religion Is Not Going Away"; Harrison, *The Territories of Science and Religion*; Harrison, *Narratives of Secularization*; and Harrison and Roberts, eds., *Science without God*.

15. Sagan, *Demon-Haunted World*, 300.

together in a complimentary way to serve the common good of humanity. Hügel's *The Mystical Elements of Religion as Studied in St. Catherine of Genoa and Her Friends* was published in 1908 and it is a massive and complicated examination of how religion works in life. It combines philosophical insights, a deep appreciation of an academic approach to religion, and psychological theory in order to try to offer an alternative view to hardline positions. Hügel wrote, "Science and Wisdom can each prosper and help and supplement the other, only if each possesses a certain real autonomy, a power to become and remain itself, and in various degrees and ways to stimulate, check and thwart the other."[16]

Hügel suggested that religion required the truth of clear, logical, scientific analysis in order to avoid simplistic answers to complicated questions: science in turn can benefit from the best wisdom that religion has to offer in order to keep science from using its discoveries in a way that will bring about harm. Science, argued Hügel, provides a perspective that suggests people share the same world and have mutual interests across ideological barriers.[17] To use science to provide clean water to a community, for example, benefits the common good. The World Health Organization today suggests that the common good exists across the boundaries of religion, race, philosophy, color, gender, sexual orientation, language, political views, disability, age, health status, place of residence, economic or social situation.[18] Hügel anticipated this broader definition nearly one hundred years ago, even if his view was not quite so broad.

Religious and philosophical belief systems need to help science consider lucidly the ethical issues that arise amid the speed of scientific advancements, said Hügel.[19] Former President George W. Bush, commenting on this issue, said, "The powers of science are morally neutral—as easily used for bad purposes as good ones. In the excitement of discovery, we must never forget that mankind is defined not by intelligence alone, but by conscience. Even the most noble ends do not justify every means."[20]

16. Hügel, *Mystical Elements of Religion,* vol. 2, 385–86.

17. Hügel, *Mystical Elements of Religion,* vol. 2, 385–386.

18. World Health Organization guidelines for human rights at https://www.who.int/health-topics/human-rights#tab=tab_1.

19. Leonard, "Hügel's Spirituality," 280.

20. Levin, "The Moral Challenge of Modern Science." A note about gendered language in quotations: throughout this book, when quotes originally used man, mankind, etc., to refer to all people, or male terms for God, I will leave the original quotation unaltered and not provide the normal (sic), expecting that people will recognize the context.

Speaking of Religion...

In our present context, debates concerning artificial intelligence, biological warfare, climate change, cloning, DNA modification, euthanasia, genetically modified foods, organ donation, product testing on animals, surgical human enhancement, and the like separate people into religious or scientific camps.

One side note: as I layout Hügel's arguments, I will streamline, and at times shamefully oversimplify his ideas, but I will leave Hügel's broader philosophical framework intact. I have deliberately left out some of his nuanced theological conceptions, which would not resonate in our time without lengthy explorations. There is much to criticize in his work as well, but I believe the main thrust of his views can offer compelling insights.

Hügel was born into an aristocratic family, and hence he is also known as Baron von Hügel, the son of an Austrian diplomat. His family moved from Austria to England when he was fifteen. Later, he became an English citizen. A devout Roman Catholic, Hügel won notoriety as scholar of religion, whose "religious world was larger than the Roman Catholic Church and included persons of other Christian and religious faiths."[21] As a result, some refer to him as a modernist theologian. In other words, Hügel saw the value of intra- or interfaith dialogue. Ellen Leonard has described him as lover of religion and truth, and one who pursued the idea of religious freedom, science, and academic rigor throughout his life's work.[22]

Hügel believed that people learn to be religious by means of a creative tension between "three elements." The first element he called the *institutional* or *historical* aspect of religious life: I will refer to this element as *"tradition."* The second, he argued, was the *intellectual* or *speculative* element, and I will call it *"teaching."* And the last he labeled *mysticism*, which today I believe is more easily understood as *"experience"* or, more clearly, the experiences we have in life dealing with the great mysteries of life.

Hügel saw these three elements as stages of human growth. He believed that people develop through three psychological/emotional/spiritual stages as they grow and seek to make sense of the world around them. Put simply, children learn about religion at first by means of traditions, which are presented primarily through the senses, or externally. Rituals help youth organize their lives by immersing them in regularized ceremonial activities, such as prayer and worship. Symbols are employed to help children begin to grasp that nature of God and reality. Teaching, the second stage, occurs

---

21. Leonard, "Friedrich von Hügel's Spirituality," 271.
22. Leonard, "Friedrich von Hügel's Spirituality," 275–77.

intellectually, or internally. Parents and religious leaders hand over the essentials, doctrinal elements of the faith, to those who are old enough to begin to mentally grasp them. Now traditions and teachings work together to give meaning and purpose to people's lives. The experience of mystery in life, the third stage, comes after the first two phases, when young adults try to come to grips with what they have learned in tradition and teaching in light of real-world experiences. During this third stage, adults may become disillusioned with tradition and teaching, if they are perceived to be rigid or uncaring. At the heart of the experience of mystery is a strong call to compassion that goes beyond one's own traditional and teaching past. Traditions and teachings give people an identity, but they also distinguish people from others. While traditions and teachings often remain deeply influential throughout one's life, it is the experiences of compassion that tends to open one up to a wider world outside of one's own religious upbringing. For Hügel, these are three ways of knowing and, since they seek the truth from three distinct perspectives, an uneasy tension results between them. Allow me an illustration to develop this point.

Roman Catholic children learn about God, which their families and church tells them is a Trinity, the "Father, Son, and Holy Spirit." Early on they grasp this concept through rituals and symbols. For example, they are taught to cross themselves when the names of the "Father, Son, and Holy Ghost" are spoken by the priest during worship. Babies are doused with water three times in the ceremony of baptism as the names of the "Father, Son, and Holy Spirit" are spoken. The images of God in the sanctuary and home suggest God is a Creator, perhaps like Michelangelo's image of a white-haired man in robes soaring in the heavens with arm outstretched and creating Adam. God, the Son or Jesus, often appears as a statue hanging on a cross or in pictures as a shepherd holding a sheep. God the Holy Spirit is famously depicted as a dove descending from heaven with gold rays of light flashing out from behind its body. Thus, their Roman Catholic rituals and symbols reinforce who the tradition says God is.

Later in life, they are taught in a Sunday school or catechism classes that the Trinity is three persons who at the same time are mysteriously only One—or God is One in three persons. A tension emerges. What the children accepted as a part of religious practice and symbols, now do not make perfect intellectual or logical sense. The church elders don't hide this fact: they readily admit that God is an infinite mystery and can't really be described with finite language. The youth accept such teaching in part because metaphors are used to help them grasp complicated concepts. The priest or their parents might tell them, "God is like water which can be fluid, gas, or ice: one in three and three in one."

The deepest mysteries of faith do not make any reasonable sense per se, because they are wondrous and beyond human understanding, and yet somehow, by means of tradition and teaching they are known through the senses and intellectually to a small degree. If youth question the logic of the Trinity, their priest or parents will tell them to trust the Bible, the authority that reveals God to be triune.

As youth get older, a tension can emerge intellectually as they struggle to puzzle out such ideas. Often in high school or college, students come to know people of other faiths, like Jews or Muslims, who are also monotheists, but who clearly talk about God differently. Jews and Muslims find the idea of a Trinity to be polytheistic. The Roman Catholic youth may wonder if they all believe in the same God or not. They in turn may meet atheists who argue that any belief in God is like chasing after fairy tales.

Experiences with other traditions and teachings happen as adults move out into the world beyond their tight inner circle of childhood community. Life experience creates a dynamic tension in faith. All may wonder, "What claim do I have to the truth over and against others?" For Hügel, these conflicts are not only natural but healthy. In fact, encounters between the three elements should act like a checks-and-balances system, which calls people back to the heart of what is truly important, says Hügel, namely the idea of loving God, community, self, and creation in everyday life experiences.

In my reworking of Hügel on this point, I would add that I believe the three elements are also true for atheists and agnostics as well, but rather than having a love of God for their highest and best ideal, they often have an ultimate concern that encourages them to live compassionately in community. (More about the idea of an ultimate concern will be discussed in chapter 6 on "Creating Conscience: Discovering Self"). Atheists and agnostics are raised with specific traditions and teachings that shape their worldviews and they too experience the wonder of compassion and awe in a variety of ways.

Hügel warns, however, when people root themselves too much in one of the three elements, life can fall out of balance at best and become dangerous at worst. In order to explore how this can happen, I will examine each element more closely and talk about the element of peril hidden therein as Hügel defines it.

Since all people are born into a specific tradition, a definite religious or philosophical context, they begin to understand the world unconsciously. Grandparents, parents, and their community hand over their thoughts about God and the religious life—even if they do not believe in God—through the senses, often before children are aware of what they are doing. This happens primarily by engaging outward rituals, practices, and symbols. Tradition is literally the first way that we are told how the world works.

Modern research has supported Hügel's conviction that we innately long to find meaning in our lives, even before we can think clearly about what this means. Andrew Newberg, a neuroscientist,[23] and Mark Waldman, a faculty member at Loyola Marymount University, who teaches about mindfulness, have written, "We are born to believe because we have no alternative. Because we never get outside of ourselves, we must make assumptions—usually a lot of them—to make sense of the world."[24] Newberg and Waldman's colleague Eugene d'Aquili, a research psychologist who specializes in studying religious communities, even goes so far as to say that we humans are "naturally calibrated to have and embrace spiritual perceptions by the neurological architecture of our minds."[25]

Paul Tillich (d. 1969), a Lutheran theologian, has argued that everyone has an "ultimate concern" that gives their lives meaning and focus. People cannot but help to hand on such convictions to their children by modeling actions and showing symbols to their children. Such concerns may be conscious or unconscious, says Tillich, but they still move us nonetheless to belief and actions. For Hügel, we learn the traditions of our parents, and in so doing are usually connected to specific institutions—a Christian denomination, a Jewish religious movement, a Muslim mosque, a Hindu temple, and so on. No matter what context we are raised in, traditions shape our understanding of reality, whether we are overtly religious or not.[26]

For example, when Christians celebrate Christmas, they will eat certain foods, often of ethnic origins, which tie them to their ancestral roots.

---

23. Newberg is also the director of research at the Myrna Brind Center for Integrative Medicine, adjunct professor of religious studies and associate professor of radiology at the University of Pennsylvania School of Medicine.

24. Newberg, *Why We Believe What We Believe*, 7.

25. Newberg, *Why We Believe What We Believe*, 7.

26. Tillich, *Dynamics of Faith*.

Speaking of Religion . . .

In my home, of German Russian origin, the tradition was to have a Christmas goose. After we lived in the USA for a while, we adapted to Turkey. Norwegians may eat Lutefisk or Torsk. Everyone has their favorite sweets, often again of ethnic origin. Tradition identifies children not only as Christian but also as belonging to a particular background.

Muslims may break the fast of Ramadan with the Eid ul-Fitr celebration by putting on their finest clothes and gathering with their family and friends in richly decorated homes. Jews have wonderful meals and rituals surrounding the Passover feast. Hindus, Sikhs, and Jains in their own ways celebrate Diwali, the festival of lights on the beginning of the new year. And there are traditional variations in all these groups as well.

Those who are raised in atheist homes also develop traditions and rituals that inform the way they make sense of the universe. In this case, these traditions reinforce their beliefs that God does not exist. Outside of openly religious contexts, people may emphasize a particular lifestyle centered on serving society through work, community and volunteer organizations, or other activities. Ritually, in the United States, they may gather regularly on Thanksgiving or the Fourth of July, besides having a secular Christmas. There are specific rituals they do that they would miss deeply if they could not participate in them. At times, even sports can become a revered focus that is dedicated to improving the individual and bringing community together. The origin of the word "fan" comes from the word "fanatic," which derives from the word *fanaticus*, which in Latin means "someone inspired by the gods." *Fanaticus* ultimately originates from *fanum*, which is Latin for "temple, shrine, or consecrated place."[27] Ritual meaning making is not reserved just for the overtly religious.

The word "tradition" originally comes from the Latin *traditio*, which means "to hand over." G. K. Chesterton once said, "Tradition is democracy extended through time. Tradition means giving the vote to that most obscure of all classes, our ancestors. Tradition is democracy of the dead. Tradition refuses to submit to the small and arrogant oligarchy of those who are walking about."[28] The ancient word *traditor* derives from *traditio* as well, however, but in this case, it means people who hand over something that they are not supposed to, such as secrets to an enemy. Traditions—cherished practices and rituals—are handed over to children quite

27. Online Etymological Dictionary at https://www.etymonline.com/search?q=fanatic.

28. Chesterton, *Orthodoxy*, 66.

naturally, because we do them out of habit and find comfort in them. Why wouldn't we want to hand that onto our youth? That is why it feels so tragic if children happen to abandon the traditions of their parents; it feels like betrayal of the past and embracing another way of living.

Religious families often take their children to specific sacred spaces like a church, synagogue, mosque, temple, or a meeting house even before they can ever hope to understand what is going on. There everyone is surrounded by symbols, such as crosses, Bibles, Qur'ans, crescent moons, Torahs, menorahs, icons, pulpits, altars, and a wide variety of art. If the tradition is iconoclastic the lack of art is a distinguishing factor.

In places of worship, symbolic actions also occur. People may remove their shoes before entering; stand, sit, or kneel to pray; they may have a leader who leads others in holy gestures. Sounds, such as bells, music, reading of texts, or singing of hymns also can be an essential part of a tradition. Food and drink are regularly associated with the veneration of a divine being; nourishments are consumed not just for the benefit of the body, but for the good of a person's soul. Children may be baptized, circumcised, dedicated, anointed with oil, or initiated into a tradition via specific ritual actions to demonstrate their belonging. Some venerate icons by kissing them; some are more iconoclastic and have no images in worship spaces. How one worships varies greatly as well. Some Christians speak in tongues; some make music with organs, guitars, or only their voices; some have statues; the variety is endless.

One can easily see that such practices engage all the senses, argues Hügel. Newberg and Waldman, in their scientific study about why people need religious or ideological systems, argue that such convictions "help us to organize the world in meaningful ways. They give us our sense of ourselves. They help us take action in specific ways. They allow us to accomplish our goals. They guide us in our moral and educational pursuits. They heal our bodies and minds."[29]

Differences, no matter how small, are significant and people can often look down on other ways of negotiating the world. I was taught, for example, to considered Catholics as "superstitious" because they prayed to Mary and the Saints. One of my Sunday school teachers emphasized the point when she told my Sunday school class, "We're not like them, because we pray directly to God." When I mentioned this to a Catholic friend he just said, "Why, that's just stupid. Of course, we can pray to God directly. Sometimes

---

29. Newberg *Why We Believe What We Believe*, 15.

Speaking of Religion . . .

I just like having someone else plead my case to God for me." I went home and asked my parents why we didn't get that kind of help from the saints and they just stared at me dumbfounded. They told me not to think about it too much. And, I should play more with my Lutheran friends.

In a similar way, my institution imparted to me the idea that the people who didn't go to church, especially atheists, were a sorry lot, were damned, led hopeless lives, and were to be pitied more than anyone else. Therefore, we needed to convert them, if at all possible, to our way of thinking to save them from themselves. Indeed, if I didn't do all I could to convert them, then my own salvation hung in the balance.

At the other end of the scale, an atheist friend of mine once asked, "Why do you waste your time with all that mumbo jumbo? You could be sleeping in or relaxing on Sunday morning like me." I suggested to my parents, that I needed to rest more and maybe we could skip church now and then, and my mother was completely beside herself. My father supported her, although I always felt that he thought I had a point.

Hügel argues that comparatively speaking there is very little critical thinking going on during this first stage of tradition. We learn important lessons externally through the senses, but children simply believe and accept what their guardians present to them. Elders are the primary interpreters of the tradition, but as children get older and become more intellectually capable, they require a more complex view of the world, and it is then that they are introduced to the teachings of the tradition.

Hügel points out, however, there are dangers associated with the stage of tradition. Sometimes people get stuck and think that traditions is all there is to religion. Such folk can become overly sentimental or stunted by simplistic ideas. In extreme cases, superstitious or delusional attitudes about clinging to a particular tradition can become exclusivist and turn people from caring for others into being fearful and hateful adversaries of those who do not hold to the real truth, namely theirs. They may say something like, "Unless you belong to my tradition, you are going to burn in hell." Religion in this instance is reduced to cheerleading for one's own team.

Teaching, the second element or stage, helps youth to think more internally, intellectually, critically, and independently about their beliefs. After an authority hands over the tradition, devotees desire to make sense of their beliefs in a more serious way by means of reason. For example, Christians hold to the Bible as a key authority of their faith, and so at this stage many will now start studying it in earnest, perhaps even reading it privately as a devotional exercise. As they do, they will inevitably run into troubling texts that have not been talked about until this point.

Children are told stories in digestible ways. Noah's flood is about all those cute animals on the ark. But once students read that text carefully, new questions emerge. Did God really produced a flood to destroy all life on earth? Okay, even if we accept that the adults were bad and deserved it, what about all those innocent children? And all those animals? How could a loving God do such a cruel thing? Youth begin wonder about how to make sense of it all.

Sacred texts have hard passages that mention violence, murder, situations of sexual abuse, or other troubling issues. King David, a hero to those who see the Hebrew scriptures as holy, manufactured Bathsheba's husband's death so that he can marry her. Moses, the Bible unabashedly tells us, was a murder. The apostle Paul, in the Christian scriptures, held the coats of those who stoned Stephen the first martyr. These are difficult revelations. When they appear, tradition is not usually abandoned, but it is examined with a different set of eyes. For Hügel, this is not only natural, but a very good thing. A normal tension develops. Youth begin to ask obvious questions that teachers have a hard time answering.

As time goes by, Hügel suggests, youth must come to grips with their beliefs intellectually. They will either cling to their traditions in some form or reject the doctrines of their faith in part because of their intellectual examination of it. What is important for youth to do, however, is for them to examine and even challenge the traditions and even the teachings that have been handed over to them by their parents and authorities, so that they may be informed followers of their faith or worldview.

As youth get into secular higher educational settings, such as high school or college, varying convictions begin to interact in and outside of the classroom. Youth may feel the desire to defend their convictions over and against others they are encountering outside of the safety of their home tradition. Often such engagement gets them thinking outside the box.

Curiosity creeps in. An inquisitiveness about what others believe and why others think and act differently can be a very freeing or a terrifying experience. It may lead to a sense of retrenchment and closing off from the outside world. Or it may feel liberating. Youth must determine parameters: does their tradition allow for them to be friends with different types of Christians, Muslims, Jews, or atheists?

Speaking of Religion . . .

One youth told me that she felt it was paramount to convert others to Christianity and as a result she went on numerous mission trips to Central and South America. I wondered who she was converting since most people there were Roman Catholic, and thus Christians. She said, "Oh, but they haven't accepted Jesus as their personal Lord and Savior. They think being baptized as an infant is good enough, and I have to show them the proper way to God." I asked what the proper way was. She said, "Being Baptist." Years later, we had the chance to talk again, and upon further reflection, she admitted that the trip had changed her, but now when she thought about it, she was no longer sure of her real motivations. She had come to see Roman Catholics as Christians, and as a result she began to wonder if converting Christians from one denomination to another was really evangelism or even appropriate. She confessed, "I know now that I was just trying to turn them into American Baptists. I was not only converting their religion but their politics. Only in hindsight do I realize that I was asking to give up their identity as (Central/South American) Roman Catholic Christians." Upon further reflection, she added that a strong aspect of her original concern for going on the trip had been to reach out to the poor. But even in this she now puzzled over the value of religious groups spending tens of thousands of dollars on airfare, to go on what she called, "a religious tourism trip" when that money could have been put to better use feeding the hungry, clothing the naked, and providing good housing.

Hügel similarly pointed out that the assimilation of political and economic opinions into religious and ideological worldviews often occurs during the teaching stage. As youth become more intellectually savvy about their beliefs, they naturally begin to embrace the more subtle political aspects of their tradition's ideology. Many religious traditions are closely enmeshed with political convictions. For example, in American civil religion, some conservative Christian traditions hold to the idea that capitalism is an extension of their faith tradition and that any type of criticism of the USA and the free-market system is tantamount to an attack on Christianity. Often, but not always, these Christians are Republicans. Likewise, some mainline Christian denominations align themselves with liberal political and social justice practices; they are often Democrats. This is true of other religions beyond Christianity as well. Most religious traditions have a range of political extremes within one tradition. This causes tensions. How does a religious leader preach to both conservative Republican and liberal

Democratic Christians concerning an issue as complicated as gay rights? Many simply avoid controversial subjects to keep the peace.

Another danger inherent in the teaching stage, suggests Hügel, is that an overemphasis upon reason also can lead to a cold, hard, shallow, and emotionless faith. Dead rationalism, which focuses upon intellectual truth or a specific set of fundamentals, can set up a theological arrogance, which can lead adherents to looking down upon others with judgmental eyes and unforgiving hearts. Extreme versions of such views may even justify fear and hatred of others because others simply do not "believe" the same way. Some even argue that they hold the only truth and others are condemned for not believing it. The implications of such rigid convictions have at times led to some of the worst atrocities that religious or philosophical convictions have perpetrated in the history of humanity. The Reich's Church, which was propped up as the official church in Nazi Germany, supported Hitler's policies against the Jews. That is an extreme example, but it is enough to make this point. Any intellectual enterprise that raises itself up and condemns others, and allows fear and hatred, can only be one step away from violence. The true heart of any compassionate religion calls for its adherents to love their enemy; this is not easy, but as a tenet of faith, it is essential of any religious tradition is to avoid the horrors of the past.

Hügel believed that these first two stages need each other to provide a fully rounded religion, but these stages also have a natural tension. As young adults seek to exert their independence, they may question why they need to participate in certain rituals, like going to church, mosque, or synagogue, or at least why they need to go so often. If a specific faith community becomes rigid, they may wonder where the love has gone and call out their own tradition and its teachings as uncaring. In some cases, they will find such tensions too hard to reconcile, and they will find another faith, or simply abandon religion all together. It is quite common in my classes, when I ask students what their religious background is, for them to say that they are a "lapsed _____" (Christian, Muslim, Jew, Hindu, Buddhist, etc.).

Many people who speak about religion, and especially the ASR, think that tradition and teaching are all that there is to religion. Here is where Hügel's insights take on a fresh and helpful nuance with the third element, experience. Hügel called the third element "mysticism": he believed that people who embraced the more experiential side of faith then were "mystics." But what worked over a hundred years ago as a term can be misleading today. Mysticism nowadays can be associated with tarot cards, crystal balls, or magic. That's why I prefer to use "experience" when defining this element.

Another problem with the term "mystic" is that it implies that these people have visions or powerful encounters with God, angels, or saints. Hügel defined the terms in a different way. By mysticism he meant the encounter with the wonderful mysteries of life, especially experiences focused on love. Mystics for him were people who called all people, those inside and outside of their religious or philosophical tradition, to being more compassionate towards God, each other, and creation.

After we have developmentally moved through the phases of tradition and teaching and have developed a system of meaning-making about the world, we then come up against the hard realities of life, which complicate our neat traditions, beliefs, and moral systems. Ethical dilemmas and tensions naturally arise, says Hügel, and become apparent when we have to reconsider what we've learned from our traditions and teachings. In other words, lived experiences may find the easy answers of tradition and teaching inadequate in light of real-world problems. Hügel believes that human experiences call religious and philosophical systems back to their core convictions, namely that true religions cannot promote hatred, and demand love. I would argue that this is true for non-religious people as well: the highest value of any non-religious philosophical system also has always been compassion.

We have already shown how Hügel believed that there was danger in focusing too narrowly on traditions and teachings in a way that promotes fear, hatred, and even violence against those who are different. Such attitudes, argues Hügel, which manifest themselves in oppressive injustice cannot be reconciled with the core elements of any religious or philosophical system. Loving God, others, and the world is the truest and most meaningful experience of the world, argues Hügel. Therefore, Hügel's idea of mysticism or experience is needed to expose cruel narrow-minded convictions, which can so easily develop among groups and within institutions. Hügel points out that crises of faith can occur when people discover that their traditions and teachings have not remained true to their most cherished central conviction of compassion.

Unfortunately, the history of religion and philosophical worldviews have far too many examples where harmful beliefs have led to great suffering. One brief example should suffice. The civil rights movement in the USA during the 1950s and 1960s was born out of African American churches in the south, who challenged so-called Christian congregations, which specifically refused to allow people of color to be a part of their tradition. White-only churches promoted teachings that endorsed racism, Jim Crow laws, and political candidates and parties that supported their values and cruelty. They justified their traditions and teachings by suggesting that the Bible teaches such beliefs and even openly and without shame support organizations like the KKK. White supremacy and systemic racism were and continue to be a part of every aspect of society throughout the USA, but can such ideas be Christian? Hügel would argue that this is not possible. Religions of hate are not true religions but instruments of prejudice and cruelty that must be exposed for what they are.

Dr. Martin Luther King Jr.., among others, argued from what Hügel would define as the position of mysticism or experience. Dr. King, Hügel would say, was a mystic, not because he saw visions but because he called racist Christians back to the core message of the gospel that Jesus preached, namely, to love all. Dr. King pointed out with loving and direct words that something was seriously wrong with religious and political institutions, that claimed to be Christian or caring, but at the same time justified hatred and dreadful brutality toward African Americans, Jews, immigrants, and other minorities. And so, Dr. King spoke out, marched, and organized non-violent compassionate protests as a means of waking up American churches, and the USA as a nation, from a slumber of ignorance and racist callousness.

For Hügel, this is what true mystics do: they demand that the traditions and teachings of religious institutions, when they oppress, need to return to kindness. Hügel also was quick to observe that mystics, when speaking out for what is right, were at their heart counter-cultural. They expose persecution that is inherent in the political and religious systems, and in so doing, they also put themselves at great risk. When the powers that be are exposed as corrupt by those who dare to speak out against them, the rulers and their organizations do not take this lightly or kindly. The voices of mystics are direct challenges to the authority and power structures and leaders who promote inequality. In response, it is typical for political and religious leaders who are challenged in this way to react by saying their way of life is being threatened by mystics, whom they label as extremists. This happened with Dr. King. Even though Dr. King gave many sermons condemning communism, he was labeled a communist simply because he was perceived to be challenging American values. The FBI and J. Edgar Hoover's vicious campaign to destroy Dr. King was nothing more than an attempt to silence Dr. King, and to allow the status quo to go on unhindered.[30] Leaders generally attack mystics by saying traditions and teachings are sacred and mystics like Dr. King are not only a threat, but they must also be silenced. If threats and coercion don't work, then often violent responses put down the non-violent protests, no matter how peaceful they may be. And sadly, often mystics suffer for their convictions at the cost of life or limb, says Hügel.

Allow me a short list of prominent people who would be considered mystics in Hügel's sense of the word, and what happened to them. Dr. Martin Luther King Jr.. died in 1968 at the age of thirty-nine, at the hands of an assassin's bullet, because he dared expose widespread racism in the USA. Mahatma Gandhi (d. 1948), a Hindu non-violent reformer and civil rights activist in South Africa and India, was assassinated by a Hindu nationalist. Malala Yousafzai (b. 1997), a Muslim Pakistani activist who works for women's rights and education (and the youngest person ever to be awarded the Nobel Peace Prize), was shot in the face at the age of fifteen, but survived this assassination attempt by the Taliban. Dietrich Bonhoeffer (d. 1945), a Lutheran Pastor and outspoken critic of Adolf Hitler and the Nazis, was hung in a Nazi concentration camp at the age of thirty-nine. Socrates (d. 399 BCE), a Greek philosopher, was forced to drink poison because he was accused of corrupting the youth of his day. Joan of Arc (d. 1431), a teenage farm girl and Roman Catholic visionary turned soldier, led the French against an occupying English army; she died at the age of nineteen by being burned at the stake. Prime Minister Yitzhak Rabin (b. 1922), the Jewish peace activist and politician, was shot at a peace rally and he later died of his wounds. Hügel suggests that Jesus himself would be an example of the type of religious leader who died seeking to bring the love and peace of God to all people, especially the poor and oppressed, because he challenged the Roman Empire.

Not all mystics die for their cause, but Hügel would say too often this is the result of their loving labors. Allow me here to offer a short list of mystics, who come from a variety of religious and non-religious traditions, who have not died for their cause, but who seek to make the world a more compassionate place and have been resisted by governments and religions because of their views. Jane Goodall (b. 1934) is an English scientist, primatologist, and anthropologist, who advocates for the Nonhuman Rights

---

30. I recommend two documentaries which deal with these issues in detail: *MLK/FBI* and *King in the Wilderness*, see the bibliography for details.

project, that is not only human but *animal* rights. Sojourner Truth (d. 1883) was a Christian African American abolitionist and woman's rights activist. Martin Buber (d. 1965) was a Jewish author (his most famous book being *I and Thou*) and peace activist, who was nominated for the Nobel Peace Prize seven times and Nobel Prize in Literature ten times. Tawakkol Karman (b. 1979), a Yemeni journalist, politician, human rights activist, and 2011 Nobel Peace Prize winner, who is known as the "Mother of the Revolution," promotes non-violent peacebuilding in her homeland and beyond. Nikos Kazantzakis (d. 1957), a Greek Orthodox author, criticized Christians for their lack of concern for refugees. Alice Nkom (b. 1945), a Cameroonian lawyer, fights for LGBTQ+ rights. Leymah Gbowee (b. 1972), a Lutheran Liberian Peace activist, helped bring an end to the Second Liberian Civil War in 2003. Dorothy Day (d. 1980) was a Roman Catholic founder of soup kitchens during the great depression and the Catholic Worker Movement. Rigoberta Mechú (b. 1959) is a Roman Catholic Guatemalan K'iche' indigenous feminist and civil rights activist who promotes indigenous peoples' rights; she is also the 1992 Nobel Peace Prize laureate.

If you read more about the above people, you will notice that many of the aforementioned activists rose to notoriety at very demanding times in history—such as during wars—and in very impoverished parts of the world, and out of difficult personal histories of having suffered oppression. Their experiences, Hügel would argue, moved them to seek a more loving solution to the world's problems where they lived, and even beyond.

Hügel believed that without the third element of experience—which is its own way of knowing and learning—a key check or balance to tradition and teaching would be missing. Religious intuitions (and I include atheist intuitions here) can have a tendency toward sentimentality, exclusivism, or rationalism that all too easily turns into a rationalization of hatred. As a result, religious groups have and sadly will continue to oppress outsiders rather than love them. By recognizing the value of experience, or what Hügel calls the emotional and psychological element of faith, as a valid aspect of religious understanding, people who believe in a divine being can return to a real love of God, neighbor, and creation by setting aside judgmental and parochial worldviews. The same would hold true for atheists, who can allow the wonder and mystery of life to help them appreciate others who hold differing views without looking down upon them for such beliefs.

Newberg and Waldman in *Why We Believe What We Believe* also talk about how human experience affects peoples' views of life. They propose that "beliefs are always in flux, and that the human brain is continually imagining and intuiting alternative perspectives on reality. This flexibility may have evolved to allow the brain to adapt its thinking to the new and unusual situations it encountered."[31] Hügel would agree and add that experience, which focuses upon matters of the heart, is where the call for positive change arises. Traditions and teachings over time can run afoul of their best intentions. Charismatic leaders, who appear to be honorable at first, can turn into tyrants who abuse trust. Institutions designed to relieve the sufferings of the world can be bent toward self-interests of the elite. Whenever leaders or institutions require loyalty at all costs, they lose their way. When this happens, Hügel argues, mystics must and will rise up to call the erring party back to the truth of compassion.

At some point everyone needs to make a choice between only loving one's own or loving neighbor and even the enemy, as the Bible demands. Dietrich Bonhoeffer was a young college professor when he became appalled that his own Protestant Lutheran church began to call its parishioners to an unreserved loyalty to Nazi leaders, the state, or nationality. He spoke and acted out against such egregious rejections of the golden rule of Christianity and was hanged for his efforts. Bonhoeffer believed that having an "irresistible love" of the "down-trodden, the sick, the wretched, the wronged, the outcast, and all who are tortured with anxiety" demanded he speak out, when others remained silent.[32]

Experience, Hügel argues, like tradition and teaching, also has its dangers. Sometimes people feel so disillusioned with tradition and teaching that they give up on them completely. Sometimes they slip into a simpler emotional way of engaging the world. Such emotionalism, however, warns Hügel, can lead to other types of fanaticism, such as hating those who hate others: the irony in the last statement should be obvious. Hügel says there can be a tyranny of mood when such experience reigns without the best compassionate wisdom that traditions and teachings have to offer. For Hügel, the best way to live in the world is to live within a creative tension between tradition, teaching, and experience: when they inform each other natural checks and balances occur and true love reigns.

Hügel's ideas also help to explain why religion appears to have lost some of its influence in western societies. Recently the Pew research center took a poll to determine which the fastest growing religious or philosophical

---

31. Newberg *Why We Believe What We Believe*, 43.
32. Bonhoeffer, *Discipleship*, 111.

convictions were in the United States. In their initial study, which spanned from 2007 to 2014, they discovered that the fastest growing religious persuasion in the US was the "nones," those who claimed to have no religious affiliation. This group was only 35.6 million people in the USA population in 2007 but it grew to 55.8 million in 2014. The survey used "nones" as shorthand for agnostic and atheists, or people who do not believe in "anything in particular." Christianity in the same period dropped from being 76 percent of the population to 71 percent. About one in five people said they were raised in a religious tradition, but now claimed none.[33] How does this information connect to the previous comments about Hügel?

I find that the trends mapped out in the Pew study, matches the experience of my students. Over the past thirty years, students from the Midwestern USA, which is where almost all of the students at my college come from, have become less religiously affiliated and identify more as "nones." When I explore this using Hügel's paradigm some interesting conversations and insights emerge. When I ask how many students identify as non-religious, a number raise their hands. When I ask this group what they mean by this, it is clear that in terms of Hügel's insights, they do not identify with the traditions or teachings of a specific institution. When I asked them if they are "spiritual" many say yes, in high numbers. When I ask them what they mean by spiritual, they generally say that their experiences in life have moved them to be more compassionate and less rigid than they perceive religious institutions are. They may or may not believe in a God, but they all believe in being loving people, who seek to make the world more open and caring.

After I explain Hügel's three elements, they readily identify with Hügel's element of mysticism or experience as being what they mean by being spiritual. So, it would appear that the "nones" are not all areligious; they are simply frustrated with traditional structures and rigid teachings that do not show compassion toward God, others, and the universe. This insight allows students to see the similarities they have with other students. Many can say, "I'm spiritual (or appreciate Hügel's idea of experience) but not religious (that is, they have reservations about traditions and teachings that are not perceived to be compassionate)." All of them agree that being loving is the best of what it means to be human, no matter what tradition or teaching they follow. From this common ground, a class or group speaking about religion can begin to engage conversations about religion in a

---

33. Lipka, "Religious Nones," Pew Research Center (May 13, 2015).

manner that allows them to conduct themselves with more compassionate convicted civility.

In the end, the three elements are basically three ways of knowing. Tradition starts with the senses. In this way, says Hügel, our encounter with the world is passive. He uses the example of a rose at this point. When people first encounter a rose, they smell its beautiful aroma, are drawn to the texture and color of its petals and are wary of touching its thorns. Such knowledge is foundational, but again it comes through the external senses. It is passive because the rose teaches those who encounter it as to what it is. Without basic sensual encounters with a rose, people will never be able learn what it truly is; such knowledge is foundational. The deeper the senses engage a rose the more people know about it.

After people have discovered what a rose is, they then learn what a rose means, says Hügel. After all, there is more to a rose than delightful smells, petals, and thorns. People may read stories in which roses have meanings far beyond their simple sensual concrete selves. Using reason, which helps give meaning to the rose, people might see the rose as a romantic symbol of love. Different colored roses also can have different meanings: a white rose might represent purity, a yellow rose friendship, and so forth.

In medieval England the red rose represented the house of Lancaster and the white the Tudor dynasty, and when they went to war it was called the "War of Roses." Back in thirteenth-century France, Guillaume de Lorris (d. 1238) began writing the vastly influential poem called, *Le Roman de la Rosa* (*The Romance of the Rose*), which was finished by Jean de Meun (d. 1305). Building on the idea of courtly love, the rose became a symbol for a Lady, more specifically the role and dignity of women.

Many over the ages have understood roses, especially red ones, as a symbol of love. Indeed, the red rose is unsurpassed as a sign of devotion, or the hope of such. So, in this instance, the meaning of the rose takes on significance by means of a reflection of the mind that goes far beyond the physical flower itself. Whereas the first encounter is outward through the senses, this second one is internal and intellectual, which assigns meaning to the reality.

Finally, the third aspect of a rose, for Hügel, comes down to the actual experience of receiving a rose, and the reality of love itself. A red rose sent by a lover to a beloved involves the action of attaining, giving, and receiving. There is longing in the gift, a yearning that either seeks to win over a lover or confirm a love that already exists. There is risk in such gestures; for example, there is the reality that love may not be returned. But when it is, love flows both ways. Similarly, when a rose is placed on a casket, it is more than a symbol of love, it carries with it the bittersweet reality of a love lost, though not forgotten.

The three elements are intertwined and each one needs the other. Therefore, Hügel concludes that religious or philosophical convictions cannot exist without community. To be a believer apart from a community is to remain alone. To be a Christian outside of a church is to be a Christian who lacks the great gifts of tradition and teaching. The same is the Muslim without a mosque, the Jew without a synagogue, and so forth. Narcissists believe community only matters if it serves them. However, real functioning communities seek not only to serve but help those among them to learn the value of compassionate sacrifice for others.

Hügel also argues that tradition is like grammar, it teaches people how to communicate with common symbols, words, actions, and ideas. Teaching is like language which puts the grammar to use in a way that helps individuals to understand and communicate their convictions clearly and within a context that others understand. Poetry, suggests Hügel, is experiential. When we hear a poem, it is both grammar and language, but it is experienced on a deeper level rather than just understood. Poetry has the power to move hearts and reveal what is truly important in life. For example, see how the simple words of Shakespeare from *Measure for Measure* (Act 3, Scene 1) convey a depth of meaning beyond mere grammar or words, "The miserable have no other medicine but hope." Or again from *A Midsummer's Night Dream* (Act 1, Scene 1), "The course of true love never did run smooth." Shakespeare inspires because his words are more than grammar and language, they are a poetic experience that points to truths in life that we know but may not have been able to understand before they were spoken. Poetry opens us up to a depth of experience we otherwise would not know.

Interestingly, Hügel also suggests that different religious traditions will tend to emphasize one of the three elements over others, even as all three remain a part of any compassionate view of the world. To give three examples from Christianity, he suggests that *tradition* is especially important to Roman Catholics. To make this point I ask my students in class who the current pope is. Most know immediately. However, when I ask Lutheran students who the presiding bishop of the Evangelical Lutheran Church is, or of their particular Lutheran denomination, maybe one or two out of twenty will know the answer. Why? Lutherans, like other Protestants, in reaction to Roman Catholicism's emphasis upon tradition, value *teaching* and focus on a more intellectual side of faith. When I ask Roman Catholics to tell me in a nutshell what they believe, they often cannot, saying it's just too complicated. When I ask Lutherans, they may respond, "We are saved by grace." Baptists or Pentecostals often say, "People are saved by accepting Jesus as their personal Lord and Savior." Those emphasizing the intellectual teach such shortcuts to their intellectual faith. Catholic worship services highlight the liturgy or traditional elements of ritual and mostly have short sermons. Protestant services tend to have longer sermons, concentrating on the intellectual side of faith, and place less importance upon ritual liturgies.

The Eastern Orthodox branch of Christianity places a stronger stress upon the *experience* of the faith. Kallistos Ware (b. 1934), a renowned Orthodox theologian, argues that Orthodox churches and worship are windows into heaven. The walls of Orthodox churches are covered in icons; and at the front of the church there is a visually stunning iconostasis (icon wall); people kiss or venerate the icons as they enter or leave; fragrant incense fills the church; music is key and the priest and congregation sing most of the liturgy; the experiential element of the Eucharist or eating of the bread and wine (body and blood of Jesus) is central to the service. All these elements support the view that the experience of worship dramatically is what matters to the Orthodox.[34] Thus, all three major divisions of Christianity have all three of Hügel's elements in worship, but they are unique according to their overall priorities.

In *The Sacred Quest: An Invitation to the Study of Religion*, Lawrence Cunningham and John Kelsay helpfully note, "The most general purpose of the study of religion is the development of a heightened awareness of religion's significance in human life and culture."[35] Hügel's views not only allow us insight into the human condition and religion's role in society, but our place amid them. Understanding who we are, how others are similar and different from us, and how we can interact with compassion, conviction, and civility is the loftiest goal of speaking about religion.

---

34. Ware, *Orthodox Way*.
35. Cunningham, *Sacred Quest*, 9.

2

Speaking of Religion

A Disorienting Experience

"Thirst was made for water,
inquiry for truth."

—C. S. Lewis, *The Great Divorce* (d. 1963)

"The unexamined life is not worth living."

—Socrates (d. 399 BCE)

This chapter lays out a variety of educational contexts in which people first learn to speak about religion. It is my hope that readers will identify with some of the examples that are presented. Hopefully these insights will lead to empathy for others and yourself. I will also briefly like to discuss how teachers, like me, try to negotiate student concerns in college classrooms on the ASR more specifically.

First, a question: do you think it is possible to understand the history of humanity without having a basic understanding of religion?[1] It is impossible to think of a day and age that has not been shaped by how

---

1. For more see Marty, *Education, Religion and the Common Good*, 117.

leaders—religious, political, or otherwise—have used religion for good or ill. Just think of ancient Egypt and the pyramids being burial tombs for the pharaohs who were considered to be gods. Or the Roman Empire and its emperors who were also called the "sons of god." If we look at the Bolshevik Revolution in communist Russia, we see that one of its primary objectives was to eliminate the influence of the previous official state religion of Russian Orthodoxy. Try imaging modern day Israeli politics or the history of Iran without talking about Judaism or Islam, or India without touching its religiously motivated caste system. It would be disingenuous and unreasonable to construct a credible argument that religion has not had a central role in human history over the ages. And yet the academic study of religion has at times had a hard time finding a place in the broader academy.

Today religion programs that focus on the ASR find themselves under remarkable pressure: many have been eliminated from college programs, because they are seen as peripheral. Educational institutions during times of financial hardship become what they think is more practical and narrow in their offerings, sometimes eliminating religion departments and courses altogether. Since the financial crisis of 2008, students, often urged by their parents, have moved away from the humanities in general to majors like business or pre-med in hopes of securing a sounder fiscal future. In fact, majors in the humanities and in religion have fallen dramatically, nearly 25 percent in the humanities in the aforementioned period down to today.[2] And yet, if we wish to have a full and accurate awareness of life on our planet, and the root of many of our worldwide conflicts, we desperately need to have an understanding of religion. The study of religion won't go away, and the humanities will survive, but the shift in mentality—namely a lack of concern in understanding others—is a troubling issue. The Declaration of Independence in the USA says that people have a right to "life, liberty, and the pursuit of happiness," but how can we understand what happiness is without understanding our deepest heartfelt religious or philosophical convictions? Or those of others?

How do colleges actually approach the ASR? Obviously in a variety of ways. There are schools whose goal in speaking about religion is to provide faith-formation. They impart the wisdom of specific traditions that promote the teachings of their founders. Whether in a church, mosque, synagogue, or temple, teaching the faithful about the basic ritual practices and

---

2. For a more nuanced discussion on this see Schmidt, "The Humanities Are in Crisis."

philosophies of a specific tradition is central in such contexts. But note that this is about "being religious" and very different from "studying religion" in an ASR setting. It is important to be clear about this difference. Both have their place. In a neutral setting, where people wish to speak about religion freely—such as a religiously affiliated college, public groups, or in private conversations—some at first will have trouble separating *being religious* from *studying religion*.

Some religion programs at private, religiously affiliated schools are very clear that they do in fact promote the specific doctrines of the institution's religious affiliation. In such instances, some may confuse this type of learning as a form of the ASR, but it is not. Especially when required attendance at worship is a part of their religious instruction, it is clear they are offering faith-formation. Sometimes students want this, but to be clear, the ASR as a discipline must be free of indoctrination. The classroom is not a place where people are meant to be formed in a particular faith tradition or worldview, but it is one where an open exchange of ideas about religion may be expressed in a way that allows people to see the reasons why they believe what they believe, and also understand why others might hold to their convictions. Rather, it is a place where the in-depth study of religion happens in a respectful and rigorous academic atmosphere that helps students learn about and confirm their own convictions, while at the same time affirming the consciences of others and their different philosophical views. The ASR allows individuals to dictate their own convictions, even as they study the beliefs of others, which at times are radically different from their own.

And yet, it would also be naïve to suggest that while studying religion academically students are not affected in their own personal faith lives or philosophical views by what they study. Thus, beyond studying religion as a means of gaining a heightened awareness of religion's significance in human life and culture, or wisdom about one's own or other traditions and teachings, I would argue that examining conscience is key to a productive engagement with the ASR. The idea of conscience is often not discussed in academic settings, but I think this is a mistake. The classroom where students pursue the ASR is the perfect context in which to begin thinking critically about one's own convictions.

Martha Nussbaum, talking about the value of the humanities more generally, has argued that students today need to cultivate "inner eyes" for the sake of the common good.[3] The ASR is a place where students can safely examine their innermost beliefs with introspection in a way that is hopefully enlightening and not threatening. In other words, in such study, students not only can know more clearly why they believe what they cling to, but they can even strengthen their core beliefs that motivate them to care for the world. This point is so crucial that I will return to it later in chapter 6 entitled, "Creating Conscience: Discovering Self."

In a classroom, it is important to note that students involved in the ASR are not graded on what or how they believe, but on how well they are able articulate their views, use academic tools such as writing and oral presentation, and on the effort that they put into pursuing the critical examination of religion. If a course on religion only imparts information about this or that religion, then a great opportunity has been missed to model compassionate, convicted, civil conversations that seek the good of all.

For college students in religion classes, a reason for disorientation may be that previous secondary education is their first exposure to the ASR. However, pre-college education when it does touch on religion, and it rarely does, is nearly always done in religiously affiliated private schools (Evangelical Christian, Catholic, Protestant, Jewish, Muslim, etc.). Private primary or secondary education almost always ties the study of religion to the confessional roots of the institution that supports the school; this often leans toward indoctrination rather than academic study. As one student told me, "I went to a [religious] high school whose religious affiliation was different from my own. While we were told that we were free to believe what we wanted, it was clear that the convictions of the teachers and school were put forth in a compelling and engaging way, and my beliefs were looked down upon as inferior, less credible, or sometimes just plain silly. I was also given sideway glances for not attending religious services that were encouraged." This is not always the case in religious high schools, but if my students reflect their experiences accurately, this is more the rule than the exception. Students in introductory religion courses at college can be disoriented because they expect more of the same.

For those who firmly cling to their own religious or philosophical orientations, they are disoriented by ASR because they may see any conversation about religion that does not support their ideals as misguided or an attempt to seduce them away from faith. For them there can be no

---

3. Nussbaum, *Not for Profit*, ix.

compromise—their view of the truth is the only opinion worth discussing, because in their mind it is ultimately the only way to salvation or enlightenment.

Such students are generally surprised to discover that the ASR encourages compassionate, convicted, and civil dialogue among the varying religious and philosophical views of a diverse student body. Rigidly convicted religious students at times do not want to acknowledge that there is a diversity among their own faith traditions. Christians, for example, may be puzzled over divisions among Eastern Orthodoxy, Protestants, and Roman Catholics, or even that there can be a wide diversity within these groups. Open dialogue that seeks to understand others for these learners may be excruciatingly difficult because they will feel disoriented by the frank conversations that the ASR engages in. They may even perceive the academic study as a danger and respond to the study as if it were a tool of the devil intent upon stabbing holes into the armor of their cherished convictions.

Many religion courses on college campuses study not only Christianity, but Islam and Judaism, Buddhism, and other faith traditions and teachings. Thus, some may be disoriented and react in an argumentative, sarcastic, and even openly dismissive manner when responding to professors or classmates that speak kindly about a belief that offers alternative worldviews. If they are passive aggressive, they may simply say nothing openly in class, but outside of the classroom they will say how terrible the professor and the other students are for promoting what they might call "false religions." If their frustrations get back to parents who feel the same way, a phone call or letter to the academic dean, or in rare instances the president, may soon follow. Sometimes frustrations boil over in the papers that they write. In such cases, students may expect and hope the professor will give them a bad grade for a project so they can claim that they are being persecuted for their beliefs, and so they may embrace the status of being a martyr for the cause. On other occasions students deliberately don't follow the assignment, because they don't like it, and go off on fanciful tangents gleefully challenging the professor, who in their estimation is too narrow-minded to see the truth.

The intent of some argumentative students is not to understand others but simply to shut down any conversation they don't like. They feel justified in doing so because they see their convictions as superior and the truly righteous ones—although they don't want to state this last idea publicly, because that would reveal a lack of humility. Their self-perception is that they are the ones with all the answers, while others are at best misguided and at worst enemies to be vanquished. The ASR is not about the exploration of religious diversity, for them, but about waving the flag of a certain ideology to see who will follow them into battle and who they need to attack.

With the advent of more online courses, this issue has become even more acute. Student who physically sit in classrooms tend to hold back a bit from truly expressing their deepest feelings. Looking someone in the eye humanizes us, to a degree at least, in a way that does not allow our emotions full reign. We couch our words more carefully because we don't want to come off as a jerk. We still disagree, but in a more polite way than on the internet.

As I've moved into doing more online courses, I've discovered that in classes where online discussions occur, especially in written form, students grant their feelings louder permissions. This is probably because online environments have a different culture of civility at play. Some people say some terrible things to people they disagree with online. During political seasons, people I know who get along swimmingly in normal life, often go at it hammer and tongs when they disagree on a point of political nuance over social media. It seems that this is even more the case with people who have grown up where vitriolic online conversations are allowed to flourish. Online we feel justified in vilifying others, often this is done with menacing cruelty, in a way we would not do face to face.

In a class on the ASR, the same happens when classes have online components. We should not expect otherwise. It's as if there is a default of harshness we turn to once we engage in online discussions. I've found that setting up some ground rules for these encounters, before they start, is essential to creating an environment of basic civility. That doesn't mean people won't fly off the handle now and then, they will, but at least when they do an instructor, and the class, can call them back to the basics of good behavior agreed upon at the start. I will discuss these rules in detail in chapter 4: "A Safe Space: Getting into the Hallway."

Regularly, however, when people who are argumentative about speaking about religion understand the focus of what the ASR is all about, they will embrace the goals of the class and their disorientation will lessen. Once they see that such study seeks to help them better understand themselves by broadening their understanding of religion, culture, and other people in general, they often eagerly enter into a compassionate dialogue with those who are very unlike themselves. The ASR does not always come naturally:

compassionate, convicted, and civil dialogue requires patience, humility, and an openness to each other.

Another disoriented response to the ASR comes from students of little or no religious backgrounds. Sometimes these students hold agnostic or atheist convictions. I have never had a student in the past thirty years who has argued that they have no opinions at all on the subject. Some who have no upbringing in a faith conviction come to the first encounter with a dread, however, that the ASR will indoctrinate them to a specific type of religious worldview or that a class will presuppose a base knowledge that they do not have. Some fear that their lack of religious convictions will be seen as a problem, and therefore will be easily misinterpreted if they speak up. A few may be argumentative from the point of view that they see all religious ideas as superstitious or barbaric and may even wonder out loud about the idiocy or simplemindedness of their classmates who believe in that foolish stuff. In an educational setting, they will certainly disagree with the values of a school that forces them to take classes on religion.

Not all without religious convictions, however, are averse to the speaking of religion. Ever since the Lutheran institution where I teach became more intentional about interfaith dialogue many years ago, we have been able to be more open about valuing philosophical convictions that reject religion all together. Atheists, in particular, care deeply about questions surrounding religion: this reality runs counter to many stereotypes that religious people place on them. They often are very eager to read texts with critical eyes or approach challenging topics with vigorous enthusiasm. In short, they have often been some of my best students and most enjoyable conversational partners. A few will want to torpedo the whole exercise, but I've rarely had students like this.

Disorientation concerning the ASR, however, can also come about in part because of the developmental stage a person is at when undertaking such study. Many first come to the ASR in their college years. Students who are undergraduates naturally begin the exploration of tough religious questions at the very time they are at a point where they may be very uncertain about their views on life in general, and religion specifically. Behavioral psychologists note that the college years are a time of exploration of ideas and actions, and often students struggle to understand who they are. This can combine with what mental health professionals have noticed of late: they observe that there has been a marked increase in reported mental health issues among college-aged people. Students are more stressed, struggle more with depression, and have other emotional challenges than students before the turn of the millennium.[4] When the study of religion engages real-world concerns that deal with sin, the meaning of life, abuse, death, virtue, evil, love, and the like, students dealing with such weighty matters in their day-to-day lives can become confused, depressed, distracted, or apathetic about topics being addressed.

In my class, for example, we read Augustine's *Confessions* and we spend a fair amount of time discussing the death of Augustine's close friend in Book 4. This reading and classroom discussion can at times trigger profound anxieties for students who have had to grapple with the death of their own friends or family. They may become quiet or emotional during the discussion. As a result, I always preface such discussions with the caveat that I know that this conversation may be difficult, and that students may need to deal with their emotions that well up and that there is help in the form of counseling available to them. The point is that when speaking about religion, people need to be ready to come to the aid of those of us who struggle because of past trauma.

At religiously affiliated institutions, sometimes students come to a particular college for sports, music, arts, pre-med, business, or some other program; they especially may feel disoriented by the fact that they will just have to put up with required religion courses, so that they can do what they really want. This is a bit akin to going to Thanksgiving where a grandmother asks her grandchildren to say grace when they clearly would rather not. A general apathy toward the subject or even a hostility toward a professor, or anyone more disposed to the topic, can set in. The ASR seems to be an unnecessary burden and in class they often will simply remain silent and hope to go unnoticed. When work is required, it comes in with a minimum amount of effort. However, some are pleasantly surprised when the instructor does not turn class into a prayer session, Bible camp sing-along, or advocate for an official religious belief system.

Some become disoriented in the ASR if the majority belief system of the institution or group they find themselves in is perceived to be a radically different from their own religious or philosophical ideas. Some state schools offer religion courses, but they are not required. Even here, however, if a student takes a religion course, they may fear that their varying views will be out of step with the majority of those on campus. In such instances, Buddhists, Hindus, Jews, Muslims, Sikhs, and others in a Christian context,

---

4. Doheny, "Depression on the Rise in Colleges?"

for example, will have apprehensions about such classes, usually wondering with fear and trembling about what they are getting themselves into.

At my Christian higher education institution, we recently have seen an increase in Muslim students from the area as the local immigrant population has increased. When I ask them why they chose our Christian college, they offer a variety of responses. Some will reply that it was based on the reputation of the college for a specific major, the arts, or athletics: they assumed suffering through religion would be a price to pay for getting what they want. In other instances, their families encouraged them to go to a religious school because they hoped that in contrast to a state school these institutions would promote moral values dear to them, even if they come out of a different tradition. Most college religion programs offer classes on Islam, Judaism, Buddhism, or other religious traditions and so this was also attractive: it suggested to them that our college cares about their faith. Still, some worry that being an outsider means that they won't fully grasp the concepts being presented, and thus be at a disadvantage. At other times, they are simply afraid of coming out of what they perceive to be a type of religious closet. Often, they have painful memories about sharing their views and as a result they were ridiculed due to the ignorance, bias, or racism of others.

At times their families are hesitant about their child's decision to go to a private college with religious affiliation. One student told me that she had been specifically forbidden to get a religion major or minor at our institution, because her parents, who live in Eastern Asia, feared she would convert away from her Buddhist faith. She told me, however, that she loved the ASR so much that she wanted to double major in biology and religion. I tried to talk her out of it because I was concerned that such a move might adversely affect her relationship with her family. She wondered if there was a way for her to take religion courses and get a major but to not have it recorded on her transcripts. We are working on that. Clearly studying religion is a passion for her, but a complicated burden at the same time.

The fear of ridicule when speaking about religion is real, and it can be paralyzing. It is important to be honest on this point: sadly, all too often, in colleges international students and those from diverse faith traditions are demeaned at religiously affiliated institutions before they ever set foot in a classroom. Insensitive people can and often do make fun of religions and traditions, teachings, and cultural practices that are strange to them. Such students regularly experience abuse for the convictions. When I have talked with colleagues from campuses from not only across the United States but from around the world, this is clearly a universal problem.

On campuses some not only ridicule other's beliefs but pressure them to convert to a different faith. On college campuses, this can happen on an athletic field, in a dorm, band-practice hall, lunchrooms, classrooms, student lounges, libraries, grocery stores, or anywhere students gather. Overt racism and subtle derision on and off campus can make some fear a classroom experience of the ASR, or any conversation about religion. I once asked one group of a particularly diverse group of students—meaning that they were non-Christian, students of color, international, or non-traditional students—if on our campus they had ever been belittled for their beliefs? The response was 100 percent affirmative. Had they felt the same off campus by our community? Again, all said, "Yes." When I share this with classes or local groups I speak to, they are usually shocked; they don't want to believe that such behavior goes on in their community. But students of difference are not surprised at all; it happens everywhere, and regularly, and this can be a mighty barrier to speaking about religion with compassion, conviction, and civility.

Another disorienting aspect of the ASR comes about when amid honest dialogue, ignorance is exposed in a way that is hurtful. In one of my classes, a student once asked a guest speaker from the local Jewish synagogue, "If you know about Jesus, why haven't you accepted him as the Messiah?" While the speaker handled the question with grace and compassion, the query itself is the type of accusation that might surface where open dialogue is encouraged. The underlying accusation was that Judaism is inferior to Christianity and that the Jewish speaker is clearly foolish for not seeing the truth. We need to be aware that it is okay to ask honest questions, but also that sometimes frankness exposes prejudice. When this arises in a class, the instructor will need to deal with it. If it happens when speaking about religion, everyone will need the type of grace and compassion my guest speaker had.

Another disorienting phenomenon is that people from traditions different to those of their conversation partners are at times asked to speak for the entirety of their faith. In one course a Christian student ask a Muslim student, "What do Muslims think about Jesus?" I jumped in and asked a similar question of her first: "What do Christians think of Muhammad?" The student immediately recognized that it was impossible to answer a question like this, because summing up Christian views on Muhammad could take an entire semester of class time and would demand a breadth of knowledge of various Christian sects that this student clearly didn't have. She said, "I don't even know what my own denomination thinks of Islam." There is at times a fine line between being compassionately curious about another religious tradition and unintentionally asking someone to be the mouthpiece of their entire religious community in a way that is clearly awkward and that puts others on the spot. This is especially true when a person is only a marginal member of a faith.

Healthy conversations on the ASR by their very nature raise difficult issues that desperately need to be discussed. Attitudes towards racism, sexism, gender bias, and climate change, for example, are all affected by people's religious and philosophical belief systems. When students from various traditions have an authentic dialogue, they can enjoy vigorous compassionate conversations with classmates in a safe environment of civility.

Andrew Newberg and Mark Waldman have argued that it is essential for those who enjoy speaking about to religion in an academic way to distinguish between "destructive and constructive beliefs"; if they cannot do this, they will not be able to "address important individual, interpersonal, and global problems."[5] What they mean by this is that the ASR must distinguish between people motivated by compassionate religious and philosophical ideals and those who use religion as a weapon to persecute others. The ASR is not a neutral exercise; it is a compassionate undertaking; one that stands with the oppressed against all oppressors. The ASR pursues empathy and the common good. More will be said about this in later chapters.

And so, it begins. The ASR involves great risks. It engages our inner eyes in a way that helps us to see others and ourselves more clearly and sympathetically. It opens hearts to the possibility of making daring and caring connections with people who may be worlds different from each other. It untethers minds from old tightly wound cruel biases. It pricks consciences to seek answers to the world's greatest and most troubling questions. And in the end, it clings to the hope that together we can seek to resolve the greatest challenges of our world, despite our poor track record in doing so up until this point in history.

---

5. Newberg, *Why We Believe What We Believe*, 5. Cf. Newberg, *Why God Won't Go Away*.

3

First Encounters with the Academic Study of Religion

Case Studies

"The only thing worse than being blind
is having sight but no vision."

—Attributed to Helen Keller (d. 1968)

"Fallacies do not cease to be fallacies
because they become fashions."

—G. K. Chesterton, *Illustrated London News*, April 19, 1930

This chapter lays out a series of case studies that are primarily intended to help students in a classroom setting. They are told from the perspectives of six people, who recount their fears and hopes concerning taking a class on the ASR. The goal is for you, the reader, to identify with your own feelings herein, as you are able, in order to not only understand yourself but also the others represented here.

First Encounters with the Academic Study of Religion

A brief overview of the chapter is as follows: Case 1: "A Religiously Rigid Encounter" is my own first encounter with the ASR. Sad to say, I once was an inflexible self-righteous pain in my professors' posterior. Case 2: "A Religiously Inclined Encounter" is written by Rev. Sarah Rohde, currently a Lutheran pastor. Case 3: "A Secularist Encounter" is composed by Emma Rifai, who has a PhD in religious studies. In Case 4: "An Encounter with Disability," Hannah Papenfuss, a senior at Concordia College, writes about how disability awareness affects the ASR. Case 5: "A Muslim Encounter," by Nadia Toumeh, a Muslim, who is currently studying to become a medical doctor. She tells of her experience with the ASR at a Christian affiliated college. Case 6: "An LGBTQ+ Encounter" is written by Luke Papenfuss, a systems analyst and advocate for LGBTQ+ rights.

Case 1: A Religiously Rigid Encounter

"In the past, when I was asked about what my own first experience with the ASR was, I often gave a short and not fully truthful answer . . . that is, I lied. My story is a cautionary tale.

"One day, I was a boy from a small farming community of a thousand people, and the next I was a disoriented student at Pacific Lutheran University (PLU), a private college in Washington State that was four times the size of my hometown. I had grown up in a deeply religious Lutheran home: we went to church every week and incorporated pious practices, such as daily Bible reading, devotions, and prayer into our meal and bedtime rituals. My mother was much more religious than my father, but he went along for the ride, because it was important to my mother. For a while, I delighted in intertwining my faith with sporting rituals: I prayed to have a good basketball game or to throw the javelin farther. I wondered what sin had kept me from doing so on off days. I journeyed to PLU to become a religion major with the ultimate goal of becoming a pastor. So, on the first day of religion class, I enthusiastically bounded into the room with high expectations. My first encounter with the ASR, however, was utterly stupefying.

"I stepped into Dr. C's 'Introduction to Religion' course in 1975 and was immediately aware of a profound conflict welling up within me. On the one hand, my home church, Christ Lutheran in Odessa, Washington, was for all intents and purposes what the media today would call a theologically 'conservative' congregation with loving people. I would not say that we were fundamentalists in the way some Baptists or Pentecostals are, but we shared many traits of fundamentalism. Margaret Miles, a professor of historical theology at the Graduate Theological Union in Berkeley, California, has noted that fundamentalism is not only a set of beliefs—especially the assertion that every word of the Bible comes directly from the mouth of God—but it is also a way of understanding and organizing the world. For Christian fundamentalists, there is a clear sense of what is right and wrong and thus a keen conviction about rewards and punishments.[1] That was me in a nutshell.

"What I expected walking into Dr. C's class at a Lutheran institution was a clear articulation of what I had come to believe as 'Truth.' I even half expected that he would lead us in prayer as class started and that the goal of my religion courses was to make students Christians, Lutheran if possible, and if they were of a different faith, to convert them. To my shock, and disappointment, there was no indoctrination, no justification of my views over and against others, and I couldn't figure out why.

"What I got instead was Dr. C talking about the Bible, a book that I read daily in a devotional manner, in a way that was completely foreign to me, referring to such things as historical critical method, literary and form criticism, feminism, racism, and so much more. Suddenly within me there was a distinct clash between my faith conviction, which believed the Bible text was without flaw (I had been raised to believe that the Bible was 'inerrant'), and the reality that the ASR for some time had looked at the Bible with academic tools to shed light on its meaning. Dr. C, I thought, was dealing with mysterious elements of the sacred text in a way that I considered to be coldly scientific. The ASR for me was a lifeless, sterile, and clinical-eyed examination of holy scripture. It seemed to me that the ASR had sucked the life out of the living, breathing faith that I had grown up with. The Bible I believed had shaped my traditions and worldview. Dr. C's more analytical approach seemed akin to a scalpel that was slowly cutting up my faith into bits, killing it, and me.

"If I am honest, however, I was also at the same time tantalizingly intrigued by the ASR. The idea that one could understand a biblical text better by knowing the original Hebrew and Greek words made absolute sense to me. I was completely taken by religion as an academic endeavor linguistically, but I did so only in the hope that I could make the text say what I wanted it to say, rather than letting the text speak for itself. I didn't

---

1. Miles, *Fundamentalist's Daughter*, 6.

want it to transform me by the depth of its complexity and mysterious beauty, I wanted it to confirm my ideas about the world.

"If the more academic method of studying religion proved that I was right, and others were wrong, then I was all for it, but Dr. C refused to let me denigrate others by looking down on them. I could not help, however, but believe that there was something inherently wrong with the ASR's openness. I couldn't quite put my finger on it at first. Initially I attributed the concern to a hastily made judgment that Dr. C must not be a Christian, or at the very least not a good one; I reasoned that since he clearly did not believe in the Bible the way I did, he must not be a 'true believer.' I became Dr. C's judge and I found him wanting. Notice the assumption: anyone who didn't believe what I did must be an unbeliever and in error. It was only later that I came to see these convictions as spiritual pride.

"Then one Sunday I saw Dr. C worshipping at the very church that I happened to be attending. I suddenly was forced to reconsider my hypothesis about his heathenism. While I puzzled over this problem, I eventually concluded that even if he acted like a Christian, he must somehow have lost his way, despite all evidence to the contrary, and it was my task to save him by pointing out his errors. I am loathed to admit it, but at that time I was completely convinced that I fully understood what those errors were, and that I was blessed with a righteousness of wisdom that was on my side.

"I decided on an argumentative approach. At every turn I would present an alternative, a more faith-filled view of reading the scripture to counter his academically precise views. I even found Bible verses to bolster my argumentativeness, like 1 Peter 3:15, 'Always be ready to make your defense to anyone who demands from you an account of the hope that is in you.'[2] After class, others of like mind and I talked about what had gone on that day, spurring each other on to become more heated in our daily confrontations with the ASR. Early in the semester, and this is painful to admit, we were incapable of learning anything from Dr. C, in part because we believed with much hubris that we knew it all already. Dr. C, however, thankfully did not give up on me, or others like me, and was patient with my disruptive behavior.

"In hindsight, I can see now that I was nothing more than a naïve foolish youth and that I was completely wrong about Dr. C and the ASR. My haughtiness then is something that makes me cringe now. I was nineteen,

---

2. All biblical passages are taken from the New Revised Standard Version of the Bible unless indicated otherwise.

Dr. C was in his sixties with a lifetime of compassionate teaching experience and study, and I believed I was wiser than he was. I am amazed at my own capacity for stupidity. Nevertheless, the self-righteous certainty of my actions at that time knew few bounds; I dared to confront Dr. C time and time again, as well as others with the truth of the gospel, as I narrowly understood it, by pulling Bible verses out of context and proof texting my arguments, in a shallow and narrow-minded manner. It was not my finest hour, but this realization would not come until later.

"Throughout the semester, Dr. C's subversive ideas, or so I saw them, continued to frighten me. For example, rather than simply reading the story of Adam and Eve or Jonah in the belly of the whale stories as literally historical, Dr. C had us read scholars who considered these passages to be metaphors or myths that communicated greater truths than simply whether snakes talked, or fish swallowed people whole. The first eleven chapters of the book of Genesis, according to some authors, he said, should be understood as pre-historic tales and not scientific texts that revealed the origins of the universe. I was profoundly horrified.

"If every last corner of the Bible was not literally true, if stories, like Adam and Eve, were mythic, didn't that call into doubt the credibility of the whole of the good book? It was an all-or-nothing proposition for me. Of course, I did not see the obvious contradiction in my own argument, namely that I did not, and indeed could or would not, read the entire Bible literally. When Jesus said to pluck out your eye if it causes you to sin (Matthew 5:29), he obviously didn't mean that literally. The Jewish Levitical laws? Well, that was ancient history, not something to be taken literally, unless of course a verse or two could be taken out of context and used to offer proofs for my beliefs. Then of course, they should be literal. My unconscious picking and choosing worked great for my beliefs: in this manner, I could wrestle the Bible into saying what I wanted it to say. I allowed myself contradictions in reasoning for the sake of my truth. I was a Machiavellian literalist: the end justified the means. And if anyone else did the same against me, I attacked them viciously for their simple-mindedness.

"I came to class armed with articles written by my authorities, biblical literalists, that agreed with me. The earth, they argued, was not as old as scientists claimed. Evolution was not scientifically valid and merely a theory, a ruse developed with no other purpose other than to lead the faithful away from God. Science itself became suspect if it didn't benefit me medically or some other means. In an indirect way, I made Dr. C abandon his lesson plan to focus on the so-called historical and scientific evidence for creationism. He listened, and patiently presented a variety of views in a reasoned and compassionate manner. Dr. C allowed me space. However, I missed much of what he had to teach me. I attended lectures not to be enlightened but to formulate counter arguments.

"One other issue that I was deeply troubled by in Dr. C's classes was feminist scholarship. I graduated in 1978 and feminist views were having an impact on not only *what* we talked about, but also about *how* we discussed issues. A furious debate raged in the academy and even among my teachers, in part because of the newness of the ideas at the time. Picking sides was easy for me: I sided with anyone that thought feminism went against God's design of divinely established male leadership and superiority.

"Dr. C belonged to the other camp. He was careful not to use male-centered language when referring to God or humanity. His point was that if God was truly God, then God was beyond gender, a point that I had to begrudgingly concede. He said that images like the Trinity, and the specific designation of God as Father, Son, and Holy Spirit have always been seen as metaphors, and that God had never been considered to be literally male by Christians. Furthermore, the Christian tradition also at times considers Jesus to be the incarnation of Divine Wisdom (e.g., 1 Cor 1:24). But this Divine Wisdom is presented as a woman in the Israelite Wisdom literature (e.g., Prov 8; Wisdom or Sophia, etc.). So, Jesus is Sophia-made-flesh, Lady Wisdom incarnate. This is another way to consider how Jesus embodies *all* of humanity and thus, conversations which merely focus on Jesus' maleness end up limiting Jesus' humanity.

"What was worse, Dr. C expected us to do the same, avoiding male language for God. Here I drew the line. If the Bible called God 'He' then God was "male," even if it was just a metaphor. However, I begrudgingly had to admit that there were passages where even Jesus used female imagery, like that of a mother hen, when referring to himself (Matthew 23:37). Or the prophet Isaiah on various occasions even quoted God saying that He, or in these cases She, was a mother (Isaiah 66:13), a nursing mother (Isaiah 49:15), or a woman in labor (Isaiah 42:14). Even though I was a biblical literalist, I was quite duplicitous as I ignore these passages in favor of my views.

"In another class, my English professor railed vociferously against Dr. C and others like him. He argued that the English language had historically referred to people as men, and those who didn't understand that were just ignorant. I went along with this reasoning. Dr. C instead suggested that the term 'men' when meaning both men and women was inaccurate and far from inclusive. Some, but not all, of my female classmates strongly made the case that language matters and being marginalized by male-focused pronouns was inappropriate. I had to confront my own ideas more seriously about gendered language, even if I did so with a lot of kicking and screaming. The ASR exposed me to my own cultural blindness of gender bias. Today, I require the same thoughtfulness of my students. Amazingly, I have a lot of students still who remind me of my former self.

"Dr. C had also had us read the writings of Dr. Martin Luther King Jr., and other African Americans, who demonstrated that religion, and my own Christian tradition, had often been remarkably complicit in systemic racism in the USA. I certainly did not believe, nor did I want to admit, that I was racist, but faced with the powerful Christian arguments of Dr. King, I was brought face to face with an awful reality about myself. Reading Dr. King's words was like a hammer smashing against my stony, biased, oblivious convictions. It was like awakening from a dead sleep to the morning of truth. Dr. King's words still echo in my head today: 'Moreover, we must learn that passively to accept an unjust system is to cooperate with that system, and thereby to become a participant in its evil.'[3] Something inside of me broke open, there was no putting it back together, it was an awareness that I had been wrong, and I was a part of the problem, and not the solution. I was coming to a point where I was finding it hard to live with my old self.

"When it is at its best, the ASR reveals what is in our heart of hearts—at times it is not a pretty sight. Since my college days, Dr. C's views on sexism and racism, as well as a host of other concerns like the ecological crisis, immigration, war, and so much more, remain central to the major issues of our day. In my classes, when we read about these issues in religion, especially when we discuss Dr. Martin Luther King Jr.., I still see myself sitting there in the students who at first resisted Dr. King's pleas. Many want to argue that a lot of water has gone under that bridge since the 1960s and that things have changed, things are better, so let's not talk about racism, especially in a religion class. However, it soon becomes clear—if we listen to people of color, watch the news, or do some basic research—that this argument does not hold. Can we honestly say that things are fine with race today? When unarmed African Americans, often youth, are being murdered daily, we must admit that we have a long way to go. I wonder at the power

3. King Jr., *Strength to Love*, 7.

that fear, hate, and violence still hold in our society, world, and religious attitudes. If we speak of religion in an honest, compassionate, convicted, and civil way, these issues will come to the forefront. A failure to do so, would suggest the whole enterprise is of no earthly good.

"Of course, this was one of my problems. Mine was a personal faith. Me getting right with God was the primary thrust of my beliefs, and I could not see that such a narrow-minded system allowed me to ignore problems that I didn't want to deal with. Sure, I was supposed to do the right thing. I just had never noticed, before reading Dr. King, that by focusing on myself, I missed how I was contributing to oppression by saying and doing nothing.

"Dr. C did not teach me from a pulpit or in a church, but in a classroom. He was a professor not a preacher, as he pointed out. If we think about this issue more broadly, have you ever noticed that when we speak of religion with others it often feels like some in the group are speaking from a pulpit rather than at the same table with us? How willing are you to listen to a person like this? If you are like me, you become easily weary of such pontificating where others are uninterested in me or my views.

"In my case, because Dr. C revealed my ideas to me naked and stripped of their baggage, I began to let go of my combativeness. Dr. C could have made me look the fool in front of the class by pointing out my arrogant assumptions with simple logic, but he did not. He could have exposed my passionate arguments as all bluster and lacking real substance with his intellectual Occam's razor, or simple rational arguments, but he did not. He listened, tried to understand, and even invited me to his office for long after-class conversations. He melted my icy methods with the warm tone of his voice and his caring demeanor. I'm eternally grateful to him."

Case 2: A Religiously Inclined Encounter

Sarah Rohde, who currently serves as a pastor in the Evangelical Lutheran Church in America in Chicago, explains her first encounter with the ASR as follows:

"While my first introductory religion class denotes my official foray into the ASR, I know there were some important precursors that shaped my experience of academia. I grew up in a home where church and faith were at the center of things. My dad was a campus pastor at a small Lutheran Liberal Arts College in South Dakota, and my mom a minister of music. Being part of the church was simply what I knew. At a young age, I became involved in Sunday school and children's choir. As I got older, I participated in worship, and enjoyed being involved in the typical church activities, . . . youth group, mission trips, community volunteer activities, etc. Even though my participation was a largely unspoken expectation, it didn't feel obligatory to me. I enjoyed going to church. I loved liturgy and wanted to learn hymns by heart. Even in my junior high days, when it was not cool to come to church—for sure not to dress up for church—I liked getting to see my friends of all ages. Not to mention the alluring power of the chocolate-covered, cream-filled donut at fellowship hour. Really, at the heart of it all, I loved the people, and for the most part the people loved me.

"While my childhood was steeped in all things church, what fascinates me to this day is the way in which my parents and our faith communities raised my two sisters and me to understand and practice faith. When I think about the way in which my parents nurtured faith in me, I cannot remember having many (if any) conversations about 'right' belief. We certainly talked about God, the Bible, and the church, but faith was never a legalistic thing. My parents didn't use categories of right and wrong, black and white, in and out. The only thing that was really cut and dry was that, through Jesus, we believe in a God who is with us and loves us no matter what.

"The Christian faith was communicated to me as much more than a belief in doctrine, but as a way of putting faith into practice by pursuing issues of social justice. I'm fairly certain that I believed in God not because God made sense to me or because God talked to me; certainly, it wasn't because I woke up one day and made the decision to believe. I believed in God primarily because I was part of a community that made God's love real in my life by caring for others. I grew up in the midst of a people that knew my name and affirmed whatever gifts that I had, and they empowered me to lead as best I could, encouraging me to be compassionate. They were the ones that showed up at my piano recitals and Grandpa's funeral. It was the love of our church that drew me in. And it was a love worth believing in.

"This was the faith that I carried with me to college. It was a faith that gave me space to learn and grow; it was also a faith that needed to be challenged and cracked open in order that it could be fully examined. I remember the first days of my introductory class to religion called 'Christianity and Religious Diversity.' I found them to be utterly invigorating and challenging. We plunged into the writings of Augustine and Luther, Aristotle and Dorothy Soelle (a contemporary feminist/liberation theologian). The authors and their writing drew me in. I knew that what I was reading was important, and I was grateful to be in a classroom with a professor and peers that wanted to engage these matters critically. I loved and relished the freedom to ask whatever questions came up. For me, this was the advantage of the ASR; it was a freedom that I didn't know I was seeking until it came to me. My experience of growing up in the church was not at all one of bondage or passive submission, yet I realized in the first months of college that there were questions I hadn't yet found the courage to ask, even though they lingered somewhere in the recesses of my mind and experience. There was a part of me that was afraid to ask them; I feared that they might shake the foundations of my faith, or perhaps offend those who had passed faith down to me. This made the learning overwhelming at times; I think a part of me assumed that, since I had been steeped in the church and Christian faith all my life, the study of religion would be a breeze. But at that point in my life, I hadn't given much thought to the ASR or concepts like original sin, historical criticism, literary analysis, epistemological boundaries, or postcolonial theory. This was new to me, and I loved it. I wanted a faith that was more informed and critical, and the ASR helped me to pursue it.

"If I am honest, however, I also struggled with it. I felt that at times I was losing my grip, and I wasn't sure what to hold on to. I found that, once I got going, the questions kept coming at me. When would they stop? Or how could I, amid them, find some semblance of solid ground on which to stand? How can I claim anything when everything seems up in the air? Each time I reached some sort of clarity about a theological predicament, I found another untapped question behind it. My searching for answers and quarreling with myself made me even address that dreaded question: the existence of God. I became much more aware of the evil and destruction that has been done in the name of God and for the sake of religion. I wrestled with our epistemological limitations, and therefore questioned humanity's right to make any claims about God's being and will. I even questioned my upbringing. Had it been acceptable for the church I grew up in to make certain claims about God and pass them on to me without critical reflection? Had I just naively accepted them, or was there a deeper meaning I was unable to see?

"It is odd, but I was still grateful to be venturing into these questions and dilemmas, in an environment of an introductory religion class. The questions I believe now would have come no matter what, either in life or a classroom. The ASR allowed me the ability to explore questions with fellow seekers and in a way that encouraged me to find my own answers.

"Still, it would be dishonest not also to say that there was an element of grief involved. Letting go of long-held convictions and assumptions is hard and sad work. But it is also true that once a childish faith (not a child-like faith, that's a different thing altogether) is exposed, then one does not want to go back to ignorance. Nevertheless, there was a part of me that longed to return to the simple trust and easy answers of my youth. But I had now immersed myself in the difficult task of undoing and redoing, and I wondered how I would begin (or whether I would be able to begin) to put the pieces back together. Ever since my college classes and the ASR started to crack open my shell of resistance to the complexity and diversity of the study of religion my sense of wondrous possibilities was revealed. I have been on a journey toward a much deeper rediscovery of God, self, humanity, faith, and shalom. While I can look back and see my first encounter with the ASR as a struggle, I am now very grateful for what the ASR gave me, tools to cope with a complex and remarkably difficult world. As a pastor, I need those tools desperately to help me make sense of the world's ever-changing landscape, while I remain true to my convictions and beliefs.

"I would also like to briefly mention one other issue that ASR raises from the outset. Throughout my life I had sought to reconcile my own upbringing (rooted in church) with our changing world. I wondered, 'How can I find ways to communicate truths, traditions, stories, and rituals in ways that relate to someone who has never stepped foot in the church?' Or for that matter, how can I meaningfully engage people of different faith and philosophical traditions that don't understand me or have a negative impression of my traditions? These questions aren't just about evangelism and mission (speaking of theological jargon), but they are about the limits, possibilities, the significance of language, and possibilities of compassion for others. How do we engage one another as we seek to authentically and openly communicate our experiences and beliefs?"

Case 3: A Secularist Encounter

Emma Rifai earned her PhD in the Department of Religious Studies at the University of Iowa. She holds a secularist position concerning religion and this is her story in her own words:

"After realizing that my college required two classes in religion to graduate, I was not happy. I discovered this while I was organizing my first-year course schedule and paying to attend a private liberal arts college to waste my time on stuff that I had learned in Sunday school wasn't part of my grand plan. Yes, I had attended Sunday school religiously throughout my childhood, but by the time I was considering which courses to take, my hostility towards religion was at an all-time high. I certainly had not always been so cynical about faith; I was a fairly devoted child and youth. Raised in the Evangelical Lutheran Church in America, I had embraced all the experiences associated with growing up Lutheran in the Midwest. We never missed a Sunday school lesson or a service—my mom was a Sunday school teacher after all. It was a struggle when she had me in her class—I had all the answers and got frustrated when she wouldn't call on me after every question. I was confirmed with my friends, attended youth group and Bible study, volunteered at all church events—lutefisk feeds, Easter breakfasts, and the like. If there was a church function going on, I was there. I had my questions and concerns to be sure—when I went through my Anne Frank phase, I just had to meet with our pastor to see if she was in heaven—but my faith was solid as a child.

"As an awkward adolescent, my church offered me a built-in community. Beginning to suspect that maybe I had outgrown my faith as I had outgrown my childhood clothes, I clung to it even more desperately. I attended Christian music fests, Bible camp, and youth group mission trips—wore Christian t-shirts and even chose Jesus as my speech topic in middle school. I had also become acquainted with a few kids who were more evangelical in persuasion, and the absolute confidence they had in their faith was appealing to me. I loved the thought of KNOWING. Constantly having a running stream of questions and doubts flowing through my head as I attended Bible study or listened to the Sunday sermon was exhausting. It seemed so easy for them, so natural. For me, it was anything but. And it was frightening. After all, I was reading the Left Behind series at a fairly rapid clip. What would happen to me if the rapture occurred and I was still in the very uncomfortable faith position I was in? And what would happen to my dad? Him being more of a cultural Lutheran than anything, I knew he didn't buy into the spiritual side of things—he thought Jesus had a pretty good message, but that was about the extent of it. I could just imagine my mom and my earnest younger brother being whisked away to heaven, leaving me and my dad behind. I lived in constant spiritual turmoil for most of my middle school years. In high school, however, things settled. The realization that my faith no longer fit didn't inspire the angst it had before. I still happily attended all the activities my church friends were attending but with the self-knowledge that I was participating more on a cultural level than a spiritual one. This worked for a while—it was like having my cake and eating it too. As I developed intellectually, however, it became harder and harder to pull off.

"By high school graduation, I had developed quite a religious chip on my shoulder. My attitude had shifted. I was sick of trying to make faith work for me; instead, I started to resent it. It was painful to discover that, as much as I wanted to be, I just wasn't religiously musical. The spirit did not move me, as it seemed to move my friends. While I still found comfort in the predictability of the traditional Lutheran liturgy and the singing of the hymns that had been a part of my childhood, for example, authentic inspiration never struck. And because I had so desperately wanted a spiritual experience, I felt rejected. When nothing happened—not at the music fests, youth gatherings, or Bible studies—I decided that if faith didn't want me, well then, I didn't want it either. In fact, I started to think, I was the enlightened one and everyone else had missed the boat. Really, faith and spirituality just weren't rational or logical. Where was the evidence? Proof? No. I was going to start college with a blank slate—I wasn't going to identify with my Lutheran background. With all the arrogance and self-congratulation abundant in soon-to-be college students, I began to map out my first semester of college only to discover its religion requirements. Oh, the frustration! The last thing I wanted to do was study something I had dismissed as irrelevant, superstitious, and anti-intellectual when I was finally leaving religion and everything dogmatic behind me.

"This was my attitude during the early weeks of my introductory religion class during the fall of my first year of college. I was a music major and felt that religion classes would be a waste of my time—after all, that time would be better spent practicing. At first, I attended the class somewhat indifferently. My plan was to make it through as painlessly as possible and then move on to more stimulating topics. I soon found, however, that despite my determination to dislike the class, I delighted in making my religiously conservative classmates squirm with my irreverent questions—like how fair is it to harden pharaoh's heart in the Exodus story and then punish him for it mere verses later. What kind of loving God would expect Abraham to sacrifice his child, and really, how could anyone buy into the myth of Jesus' virgin birth? At first, I asked these questions flippantly with the self-confidence that I already had all the answers. I realize now that my unexamined devotion to my secular identity was not so different from the more faithful identities of the students I was judging. Many of my classmates too felt they had all the answers—religion classes weren't for them either; they had already learned it all in Sunday school. They wanted their faith shaken as little as I wanted my secularism challenged. A few weeks into the class, however, I started to suspect that I didn't have all the answers. Instead of responding with my knee-jerk sarcasm in class, I began to slow down and really pay attention. This was, of course, a little unnerving. What if religion wasn't irrelevant? What if examining religion and faith led to insights about human nature and society? What if all the faithful in the world weren't mindless drones, brainwashed into accepting their respective faiths? It started to dawn on me that my arrogance had blinded me—maybe I didn't need a faith of my own, but I was sure starting to enjoy studying religion from an academic perspective.

"It helped that I liked my professor, Dr. L, whose class bore no resemblance to Sunday school whatsoever. She won me over class period by class period, until I could hardly wait for my religion classes. We looked at all sorts of topics as though we were working on a puzzle, together examining a piece this way and that to see how it fit into the bigger picture that was human experience. We started the class with topics that didn't particularly surprise me—the Hebrew Bible stories, early Christianity, and so forth—but Dr. L pushed us further and beyond—what about gender? Race? Other faiths? No, this wasn't simply learning and repeating the same stories I had grown up with. I began to engage. And with engagement came the questions. At first, I needled and pushed just for fun; however, soon I found I was genuinely intrigued. I had also started to suspect that Dr. L was enjoying my questions, even the snarky ones. It still surprised me, however, when she thanked me for my contributions when I met with her to discuss paper topics midway through the semester. It was then that I finally realized that maybe my questions had a place in the study of religion—perhaps with just a little less attitude. It occurred to me that instead of dismissing religion as irrelevant as I had been—a misjudgment that still embarrasses me—I could pick it up and look at it, reflect on the myriad ways it informs human experience and society, and explore how it intersected with other aspects of human life. With my discovery came humility.

"It had never occurred to me that maybe this was really what religious studies was all about and that there might be a legitimate place in the study of religion for someone like me—someone sincerely interested in the topic with no interest in developing personal faith. I had thought faith was a prerequisite for studying religion and was delighted to discover that it wasn't. In fact, the ASR has very little to do with faith identity—good religion scholars approach their subject matter with as little bias as possible, regardless of personal orientation. While faith identity isn't a light switch—I can no sooner switch off my secular worldview than can my more faith-filled colleagues—true scholarship is produced when we strive to keep these identities, whatever they may be, from influencing the outcome of our research. It is, perhaps, just as challenging for me to not let my secularism cloud my work as it is for the Christians, Muslims, and Jews. But this is the task we are afforded. And it is this approach that differentiates religious studies as an academic discipline from the proselytizing of the church—it is not the place of religious scholars to favor any one faith, or lack of faith, over another. They are not to missionize or spread the message or save souls. Their job is to examine closely one of the most compelling and fascinating aspects of human experience—religion—and illuminate, as Max Weber would say, why it is just so and not otherwise. I was only just becoming aware of these nuances as my first class in religion was coming to an end. When we received comments back on our research papers that fateful semester—I had looked at the relationship between science and religion—Dr. L. had auspiciously written 'Any chance of converting your major?' on the top of mine. And by the end of my first year at college, I was indeed a religion major."

Case 4: An Encounter with Disability

Hannah Papenfuss, currently a student at Concordia College studying Spanish and Psychology, explains that her first encounter with the ASR was influenced by her advocacy for disability rights. This is her story in her own words:

"Prior to enrolling in an introductory Religion course, entitled 'Christianity and Religious Diversity,' I felt an inescapable sense of dread. This wasn't because I was inherently hostile to religion: in fact, the opposite was true. I had grown up firmly rooted in the Evangelical Lutheran Church in America branch of Lutheranism. My mother serves as the organist and music director at our church, and my father raises money for my college. Church was and is a regular fixture in our family life, and some of my earliest memories of it are quite happy ones. I would cuddle with my dad during sermons, sometimes falling asleep in the pew. At other times, I would complete the activities in the children's bulletin with a near-obsessive level of thoroughness. The part of church that I liked the most, however, was Sunday school. It was a time during which I could learn about stories from the Bible and complete activities with my friends. In that setting, I first learned about the healing narratives of the Gospels, which would later hurl me into a crisis of faith that I have been attempting to navigate for years.

"I should preface this by saying that I was born with cerebral palsy, a condition that has caused me to require a wheelchair for my whole life. It sounds strange to admit now, but in my younger years, my disability hardly registered on my radar. Though I knew I was different from my peers, those differences didn't interfere with my ability to interact with the world on the whole. I was also discovering in church for the first time that Jesus spent time healing people who were sick or hurt when he was alive. Since he was apparently coming back, all I had to do was bide my time, and then I would be able to walk one day. It wasn't until I was about seven that I began to question the stories I had learned growing up. By that time, I was more keenly aware of the things my classmates could do that I couldn't. I was lonely, and I hated feeling left out. I slowly began to realize that if Jesus ever came back, it wouldn't be for a very long time, certainly not while I was alive. So, I started to doubt myself. What made me different than the people that Jesus had healed? Why wasn't I good enough? Those two questions, and God's silence in answering them, would fuel a kind of inner rage followed by depression that would follow me into my teenage years.

"My understanding of healing narratives, along with different ways of interpreting their meaning, gradually expanded with the help of some disability-affirming mentors. I learned how to look at them from a metaphorical point of view and how to pick out details that subverted established norms regarding how society is supposed to interact with the disabled. For example, Jesus frequently prefaced any healing act with some form of touch, which was usually taboo for a variety of reasons. Therefore, the simple act of making physical contact with someone communicated a sense of belonging and inclusion that had not been granted to a whole class of oppressed people. The way I saw it, that inclusion was far more curative than any restoration of physical or psychological function.

"The negative emotions that I had directed for so long at God suddenly began to shift to the church more broadly and the negative stereotypes about disability it continued to perpetuate. My sensitivity to the portrayal of disability issues in the Bible and worship services only heightened as I got to my church-affiliated college. As the only chapel attendee who had to remain seated for the entire service, I bristled whenever the congregation was asked to stand without the caveat of 'as you are able.' I would also give myself pep talks before a homily if I could tell from the insert that the text was a healing narrative, hoping to soften the inevitable blow of the underlying assumptions about disability and its relation to sin going unchallenged. I was slowly getting used to the idea that God might be okay with my identity, but warming up to church leadership and forgiving their mistakes would prove to be a much longer, and more delicate, process.

"It was in this context that I signed up for Dr. H's section of 'Christianity and Religious Diversity,' an introductory course to the study of religion, with a chip on my shoulder and one doubt short of a full-blown existential crisis. Thankfully, he was open to me expressing my unique perspective in class, as I was the only conspicuously disabled student. Although my classmates were generally gracious, I did sometimes have to challenge their opinions. Early on in the semester, we were instructed to split into groups based on the extent to which we self-identified as religious. I don't remember the exact context of the comment, but at one point, someone in my group remarked, 'I just feel like everything in life happens according to God's plan.'

"I debated internally whether to say something. On the one hand, believing that God has complete control over everyone's lives provides a certain degree of comfort, and I wasn't sure if I should be the one to poke holes in her worldview; that being said, people had told me when I was really struggling with my disability that it was all part of a plan, and that was really hurtful to me. Why would God plan for me to be born with a condition that would cause me and my family so much hardship? More broadly, why would God allow me to be born into a world where I would face discrimination and unequal access based on my physical constraints? I decided to point this out to my classmate by saying the following: 'If that's true, then that means that God planned my disability; in my opinion, that would make God an asshole. It's fine if you believe that for your own specific circumstance, but be careful when saying that to other people.'

"I remember her getting a little defensive, as is to be expected. If my memory serves me, she remarked that she had been really sick as a child and credited God with her recovery. In and of itself, there's nothing wrong with that. The problem comes when that personal belief gets extrapolated to include others. Because when someone assumes that God has the capability to heal anyone at any moment, it leaves those who have disabilities open to suspicion and distrust, as if the individual in question could be doing more to help themselves. It places the responsibility on *them* to heal, rather than on the church to include.

"All and all, I shouldn't have been afraid. I had the opportunity to educate my classmates about the harm that traditional interpretations of healing narratives can cause for people with disabilities and offer disability-affirming alternatives. My peers seemed receptive, or at least they didn't challenge me publicly. The girl I sat next to in class even told me once that my comments changed the way she thought about disability and God. Most importantly, Dr. H never pushed a given viewpoint on us: he encouraged us to question our beliefs and question them again. As I struggle to make sense of what it means to be Christian in a largely ableist society, he was one of the people who exemplified how to sit with uncertainty and doubt."

Case 5: An Interfaith Encounter

Nadia Toumeh, presently a graduate student at the University of North Dakota school of medicine and health science, discusses her first encounter with the ASR as a Muslim at a Christian liberal arts college as follows:

"I was born in the United Arab Emirates, but my parents and extended relatives are from the country of Syria. My family and I immigrated to Fargo, ND in 2005 due to my father's job, and have lived there ever since. I chose to go to a Lutheran Liberal Arts College for several reasons, with the main reason being that I knew how strong its pre-medicine program is. Most of all though, I enjoyed being in the college's inclusive environment. The religion classes were often where I felt this sense of inclusion, such as while learning about how the Bible was written, or what the teachings of the Buddha are. My professors were able to make all of their students feel included in the conversations, no matter what our religious beliefs were. I am forever grateful for what my college taught me when it comes to learning how to appreciate and embrace the differences that exist between us as individuals.

"More specifically, I was born into a family of Sunni Muslims, and I was raised by parents who structured my childhood in ways that allowed my religion to be a significant contributor to who I am today. Growing up in the United Arab Emirates, a country with a large Muslim population, many of my days were spent attending Islamic lessons. The lessons consisted of learning about the Prophet Muhammad, memorizing and interpreting the Qur'an, as well as understanding how to follow the teachings of Islam. The

Speaking of Religion . . .

majority of my instructors were female scholars who to this day greatly influence how I see myself fitting into the religion of Islam. The fact that I was continuously surrounded by Muslims meant that I never saw myself as an outsider when it came to religion. My naïve self at the time believed that it would be okay if I didn't really learn about other religions. This mindset changed the minute I set foot into Fargo, ND at the age of seven. My father wanted to fulfill his dream of practicing medicine in the United States, and my family and I found ourselves in a place that felt isolated from everything that we had previously found comfort in.

"The transition into the American school system had some challenges that would often leave me feeling alienated. I suddenly found myself accidentally consuming foods that had pork products in them. This was a nonexistent concern for me back home. Students would stop eating and stare at me when I wouldn't eat or drink anything during lunch hour in the month of Ramadan. They would ask me why my mother chose to cover her hair. They wondered why I had to sneak away from a group of friends when it was time to pray. At the age of fifteen, I chose to don the hijab. It was a decision that I made on a summer morning, right before starting high school. My parents were hesitant about my decision, as they were nervous about the treatment that I would receive from those around me. They were nervous that I would change my mind and never want to wear the hijab again. The questions from those around me at school began to transition into those of concern. Was I forced by my family to wear the hijab? Did this mean that I couldn't live up to my full potential? I don't always know how to approach answering questions about my hijab, especially when the person asking them seems to pity the fact that I can't show my hair in public.

"I have always made it a goal of mine though to paint an accurate picture of what it means for me to wear the hijab in the Midwest. The hijab has never hindered me from enjoying life. The hijab hasn't stopped me from playing sports, traveling, receiving an education, and so much more. If anything, the hijab has allowed me to have confidence in my ability to stand up for myself when approached by individuals who are ignorant about Islam.

"Choosing to attend a Christian college was not an easy decision by any means. I knew that I was going to be one of the few hijabis on campus. I knew that I would get placed in certain categories before I even interacted with an individual. Most of all, I knew that my religion would set me apart from my classmates. After a couple of visits to campus though, I began to see myself belonging there. And coming into college, I was quite nervous about taking two required religion courses. I barely knew anything about Christianity, but I was assured by multiple faculty that it would be more than okay. My upper division religion course with Dr. L ended up being my favorite class that I took at college. In her course, I learned how religion can be used to empower women. I learned how to use the Qur'an and other Islamic writings in order to explain to others that Islam does not oppress women. Her course forever changed how I perceive my experiences as a Muslim female. I was also interested in the school's mission to encourage interfaith dialogue, and its dedication to creating an inclusive environment. I didn't fully understand the impact of having interfaith dialogue until I attended college. Now more than ever, in a society in which we tend to look down on those who are different from us, we need to learn how to appreciate our differences. The countless times I've been afraid to take out my Qur'an to read in public have shown me just how much our society is in dire need of a shift in the way we perceive other religions. Interfaith isn't just learning about another's religion, but it's about knowing how to rid our minds of any attitudes we might have about a certain religious belief or practice.

"As I head to medical school, I'm eager to see if my experience as a Muslim female student will be any different than what I experienced at Concordia. I often wonder what my future patient interactions will be like, and if I'll ever come across patients who are intimidated of being treated by a hijabi female. In all honesty, I can't wait to have meaningful conversations with those patients, and to give them a glimpse of the peaceful religion of Islam that I cherish so dearly."

Case 6: An LGBTQ+ Encounter

Luke Papenfuss, a systems analyst at Concordia College in Moorhead, Minnesota, notes that his first encounter with the ASR at college was informed by his advocacy and concern for LGBTQ+ rights. Here is his story in his own words:

"As a gay Christian, and a freshman no less, I was mildly apprehensive to take my first religion class at Concordia for fear of what others in the class might think of me and/or my sexuality. Luckily for me, I had grown up close to the college and knew that the religion department and Concordia College were both welcoming places, so that helped take away some of my apprehension, but it did not completely abate it. I had come out publicly earlier that year (most of my friends and immediate family had been told I was gay at this point). While it was mostly an 'open secret' at that point—meaning that if anyone asked me if I was gay, I was not going to lie—I was not screaming it from the rooftops either. At that point in my life, I considered myself to be culturally a Christian, but did not really jive with religion. By 'culturally a Christian' I mean that, given that I was raised in an Evangelical Lutheran Church in America my entire life, I knew that many of the traditions and teachings had influenced me and my thinking, but that did not necessarily mean that I believed in everything the church taught.

"A class called 'Christianity and Religious Diversity' was my first foray into the world of the academic study of religion, and it was a breath of fresh air after only having experienced religion via my church, whether it be through a church service, a sermon, Bible passages, or Sunday school. Learning how to think critically about religion—heck, even being *allowed* to think critically about religion without judgement by a professor—was liberating. It was the first time that I started learning why religious groups (including my own!) believed what we believe, and it was the birth of my realization that I was allowed to come to my own conclusions regarding my religion after hearing so many people throughout my life (not at my church, but just in general via the news, overhearing conversations, what have you) say that the Bible is the infallible word of God, that homosexuality is sin, and that gay people are going to hell.

"When we were told we had to write a research paper at the end of the semester, I knew I wanted to write mine on the passages about homosexuality in the Bible. I spent a rather large amount of time writing that research paper, given how passionate I was about the topic. My academic exploration mixed with my personal questions. Does the Bible *really* argue that gay people, and I myself, are going to hell? What I discovered was how the Bible had been misinterpreted and misread over the centuries for cruelty and not compassion. After finishing the paper, I ended up also writing a letter to my extended family members that I had not yet told I was gay, and sent them each a letter, along with my paper, as my coming out to them.

"While I did not have a major declared when I took this class as a freshman, this course prompted me to take more religion classes, because the ASR fascinated me and opened up religion to me in a way I had never experienced. I later added religion as a major to my focus on computer studies. To this day, I still identify more with academic thought than the lived experience of my religion (although that's not to say I completely eschew that part of my life by any means). However, the foundational belief I hold about the Bible (that I think can easily be applied elsewhere), I discovered thanks to one of my religion professors, Dr. C, who is a biblical scholar. My senior year he said something along the lines of 'any interpretation of the Bible that belittles, marginalizes, oppresses, or harms another person is a bad interpretation.'

"That statement from my professor is vital to me because of how many LGBTQ+ people have either felt, or literally been, excluded from church, religious life, and even family and friends, due to certain religious beliefs. While great harm has been done to LGBTQ+ people in the name of religion, it heartens me to know that many in the LGBTQ+ community have become religion majors or become involved with religion in some way. And it makes sense. After a lifetime where they likely never experienced the ASR, they encountered in such class the opportunity to ask questions, to challenge the status quo, and to believe freely.

"I think a number of students, after taking the required religion courses sometimes end up unsure of what they believe, or if they even believe anymore. I think this can happen with anyone, but I suspect that it is more often the case for those who feel absolutely certain about their beliefs. I think that being unsure of what they believe, or even if they believe, is good! I think that it means that they were forced to think about their beliefs critically, which means that some of their beliefs were challenged, and that some of them changed. However, I think too often the students that this happens to fail to realize that it was simply some of their beliefs/conceptions/ideas of religion that were problematic, and it is not that they are necessarily no longer religious (although that may be the case for some).

"Interestingly enough, I feel like this is what LGBTQ+ people go through at an even younger age—pretty much as soon as they realize that they are, or even might be, gay. They often grow up having either experienced, or at least heard of, negative conceptions of LGBTQ+ people, and have been forced to challenge such beliefs, leading them to either abandon religion or struggle to stay, or to keep those beliefs and deal with some massive amounts of self-hatred. In my case, while my church never said anything negative about LGBTQ+ people, when I was young, they also never really said anything positive about LGBTQ+ people either, so I did not really know where my church stood.

"Today, my church is far more intentional and is in the process of becoming a Reconciling in Christ congregation, which denotes that we are explicitly and publicly welcoming of LGBTQ+ people, while remaining a congregation of the ELCA. But when I was younger and my church was less intentional, that feeling of being uncertain about where we stood on the topic of LGBTQ+ people, let alone without clear and public support for other marginalized individuals, made it easy for some of the louder more anti-LGBTQ+ Christians to seem like the predominant viewpoint in Christianity. So, while that may have easily *seemed* like the predominant viewpoint in Christianity to many of us LGBTQ+ people growing up, anyone like myself that got involved in the ASR was taught just how incredibly diverse Christianity is, let alone other religions, and it helped us learn how to academically think about such topics so that we could come to our own conclusions.

"This leads to one of the best, most helpful parts of the class, which was also somehow simultaneously the most annoying and angst-inducing part. My professor, Dr. H, would never tell you exactly what to think unless it was a fact (such as if someone asserted that the Bible says ____ on ____ topic, when in fact, the Bible never mentions said topic whatsoever). Instead, he'd ask leading questions, nudging you to talk out loud through your thoughts and/or issues, and somehow eventually, even if it took a while, force you to come up with your own conclusion. The only time you'd know or even get a whiff of what he might think was if someone mentioned something that, as Dr. C said, 'belittles, marginalizes, oppresses, or harms another person'—he would make *that* known.

"I think that the method of pressing students to reach their own conclusions, while simultaneously informing them when their beliefs have the capacity to harm another is what really gets to the heart of the ASR. It is emblematic of how vital it is to have the ability to think critically about our ideas, actions, and words in a world where it is much simpler to never do so."

Concluding Thoughts

The fears, perils, challenges, and joys of the ASR are evident in the preceding encounters. In academic settings, students often enter into the enterprise of studying religion with much trepidation: they do so, however, from many different angles. As the struggles begin, assumptions are made, sides chosen, and often there is a considerable amount of resistance due to fear and misunderstanding. However, once false perceptions are slowly set aside, the challenges of the academic study may be embraced with enthusiasm. Much like learning a new skill, language, or sport, the ASR takes practice and dedication as well as compassionate, convicted, civility.

4

A Safe Space
Getting into the Hallway

"There is no conversation more boring
than one where everyone agrees."
—Attributed to Michel de Montaigne (d. 1592)

"In conversation, humor is worth more than wit
and easiness more than knowledge."
—Attributed to George Herbert (d. 1633)

If speaking of religion is disorienting, then what do we do? Since the perplexity primarily develops out of a fear that others will lack compassion, conviction, and civility towards us when we speak our mind, we need a safe space where we all can share without fear of reprisal. Allow me to borrow a metaphor from C. S. Lewis that demonstrates how a safe space might work. Lewis suggests that speaking of religion is best done when we all "get into a hallway," a place that exists between our differences—that is the rooms where we normally live out our religious/philosophical lives.

Speaking of Religion...

During WWII, as Nazi bombing raids hammered London, the English people wondered how such evil had become a part of daily life. There seemed no end to the madness, and spirits over England were quite low. The British Broadcasting Company tried to offer their listeners some hope, so they enlisted C. S. Lewis, a popular author and speaker, to give a series of radio broadcasts to speak to these issues head on. From 1941 to 1944 Lewis presented his reflections over the airwaves and these addresses were later gathered into a book entitled, *Mere Christianity*.

In the introduction to the book, Lewis notes that he wished to talk to the British people directly, but this was a challenge because there were numerous divisions among them. Lewis directed his message primarily at Christians, who were Anglican, Roman Catholic, Methodist, Baptist, and the like. Lewis, himself an Anglican, noted that sometimes differences of tradition or teaching hindered meaningful conversation and compassionate understanding. He told his audience that he wanted to talk about what unified, rather than divided them, or what he called "Mere Christianity," in order to foster courage and community.[1] Lewis noted specifically that he was not interested in converting others to his views, they all had their own consciences after all, but rather he hoped to open a dialogue that would help the people of England work together amid the horrendous trials of the day.

I find the illustration useful. But clearly the hallway metaphor reflects Lewis's Christian context and audience. I will, however, adapt and broaden the example beyond Lewis's original setting in order to make a wider claim about all religious and philosophical traditions. But first, let us look at Lewis's own explanation of the hallway. Lewis writes:

> I hope no reader will suppose that [a conversation about] "mere" Christianity is here put forward as an alternative to the existing communions—as if a man could adopt it in preference to Congregationalism or Greek Orthodoxy or anything else. It is more like a hall out of which doors open into several rooms. If I can bring anyone into the hall, I shall have done what I attempted. But it is in the rooms, not in the hall, that there are fires and chairs and meals. The hall is a place to wait in, a place from which to try the various doors, not a place to live in. For that purpose, the worst

---

1. Lewis borrowed this idea from Richard Baxter (d. 1691), an English Puritan, poet, theologian, and prolific author. Baxter encouraged his readers to focus on the essentials of Christianity, namely the compassion that Jesus offered and taught, and to avoid divisions that developed out of sectarian rigidity. For more see Keeble, "C. S. Lewis, Richard Baxter, and 'Mere Christianity,'" 27–44.

of the rooms (whichever that may be) is, I think, preferable. It is true that some people may find they need to wait in the hall for a considerable time, while others feel certain almost at once which door they must knock at. I do not know why there is this difference, but I am sure God keeps no one waiting unless He sees that it is good for him to wait. When you do get into your room you will find that the long wait has done you some kind of good, which you would not have had otherwise. But you must regard it as waiting, not as camping. You must keep on praying for light: and, of course, even in the hall, you must begin trying to obey the rules, which are common to the whole house. And above all you must be asking which door is the true one; not which pleases you best by its paint and paneling. In plain language, the question should never be: "Do I like that kind of service?" But "Are these doctrines true: Is holiness here? Does my conscience move me towards this? Is my reluctance to knock at this door due to my pride, or my mere taste, or my personal dislike of this particular door-keeper?" When you have reached your own room, be kind to those who have chosen different doors and to those who are still in the hall. If they are wrong, they need your prayers all the more; and if they are your enemies, then you are under obligation to pray for them. That is one of the rules common to the whole house.[2]

Lewis's obviously Christian point of view comes through loud and clear, and at this moment some of his language may be off-putting to some readers, who wish to speak about religion. Nevertheless, I believe we can reconsider the idea to set up a more contemporary framework for fruitful conversation around the ASR, in or outside the classroom.

Students in an introductory course on the ASR, for example, come to the hallway of the classroom from a variety of contexts, rooms, where they live out their religious or philosophical lives. Lewis's suggestion that some people are stuck in the hallway at times, seeking but unable to find a comfortable place to rest their hearts and/or minds, reflects how things are at times. Some live in Roman Catholic, Orthodox, or Protestant rooms; more broadly speaking others live in chambers with atheists or agnostics; still others are Muslims, Jews, Hindus, Buddhists, or another religious tradition. But no matter who we are, the classroom can be compared to a hallway where all gather for a short while to have open, compassionate, convicted, and civil—even passionate—dialogue about questions of great importance. Besides the classroom, the hallway may be an adult study

2. Lewis, *Mere Christianity*, xv–xvi.

group at a religious institution, interfaith conversation, or a casual conversation in a coffee shop with a friend, a family gathering, and so forth.

The hallway is a place where we explore our consciences and seek truth, even as we may vehemently disagree with one another. I would also argue that the hallway is not only a space for the living but can include ancestors. When we read religious authors from the past, we bring their voices into our hallway conversations so that we may learn from them. In the hallway, if we pause, listen carefully, and engage empathetically, we can hear the echo of conversations of the past mingle with our voices. In so doing we can build upon the wisdom of the past to construct a better future in the present moment by means of the ASR.

After encounters in the hallway, we all go home to our own rooms of conscience with people of like mind. The lodgings are comfortable places with fires and food that are to our liking, for the most part. The questions that were brought up in the hallway inform our conversations in our rooms as well. But in the hallway it is not our task in the ASR to convert someone else to our position. There we encourage others and even ourselves to discover what our consciences tell us and why. This can only be done if we understand our own convictions more fully, as well as appreciate and value others' right to self-determination.

In a way, when we look at people with different religious beliefs, they become like a mirror reflecting our best and worst traits to us. When we are in a room with like-minded individuals, we take for granted our traditions, social norms, and our belief systems; we overlook our own narrow-mindedness or flippant insensitivities, overlooking them because it's hard to notice them when others don't realize they are issues. The "in crowd" all too often sees those outside their group as strange. Insiders at times will even make jokes about outsiders and not even realize that they are being racist, sexist, xenophobic, or insensitive. When this happens, we turn those outside of our circle into the "other." Ironically, however, when we find ourselves to be stereotyped, we object and claim that we have been misunderstood and that "they" are thoughtless. However, it is also true, that if we ever find ourselves in a cultural context where we are in the minority, outside of our comfort zones, we will be able to see things about ourselves that we never noticed when we were in the majority.

Allow me an example to make my point. The first time I traveled to Istanbul, Turkey I was awakened early in the pre-dawn morning by sung prayers pouring forth from public address systems of minarets. Istanbul is known as the city of a thousand mosques, and since prayers sang forth from each one, they echoed from all directions. The prayers were impossible to sleep through. At the outset I was puzzled at what seemed like noise and then I marveled at what I heard: I listened transfixed at their beauty until they faded. I wondered, "Are the Muslims who live here awakened every morning by such prayers?" "How many Muslims actually rise early for these prayers?" I asked a Muslim guide later in the day these questions. He said, "Oh no. We are used to the Adhan, but I sleep right through them. Some rise for prayers. They are better than I." For Muslims in Istanbul, this is a part of the room they live in, but outsiders will be unsure of what to make of all this.

On my first tour of the magnificent Blue Mosque, I entered the Muslim worship space tentatively, uncertain of the protocol. I like other non-Muslims had to learn the rules. I had to remove my shoes, to make sure my legs and shoulders were covered, to move quietly and respectfully through the sacred space, and so forth. I observed that Muslim prayer practices had their own unique style; they knelt, bowed, and stood facing in the direction of Mecca. Such ritual was completely unfamiliar to my own prayer practices. These customs were the religious air they breathed, but for me I felt short of breath, so to speak, both out of uncertainty and awe. It was as if I had walked into someone else's room and I bumped into the furniture, because I was unfamiliar with the space.

Sacred places have ceremonies that need to be learned. For the insider, they are as easy as eating a meal with family; for the outsider they are as awkward as learning a new language. As we enter into the places of different religious cultures, we begin to see ourselves and our own religious ideals more clearly because we are forced to evaluate them in light of the similarities and differences around us. Muslim sacred places and practices in Turkey became a mirror that showed me myself.

For those of us who have the privilege of travel, or simply the ability to encounter varying religious traditions in our own communities, engaging difference and similarity can be of great benefit. As I got to know Muslim religious culture better, I began to experience what Barbara Taylor Brown calls "Holy Envy."[3] During the aforementioned trip to Turkey, I wondered why, for example, my religious tradition put less emphasis upon posture during prayer. Muslims prayed with their whole bodies; I prayed only with a slight tilt of the head and maybe folded hands. It seemed to me that

3. Taylor, *Holy Envy*.

there were many benefits to such practices that I was missing out on. But I wouldn't have noticed this without looking into the mirror of difference. By visiting the Muslim room, I was greeted with the hospitality of compassionate comparison that helped me to begin to notice and engage Muslims in the hallway with a new appreciation. How terrible it must be, if we refuse not only to enter the hallway, but to lock ourselves up in our own rooms, ignoring the world around us. Can such people ever know themselves when they only look in mirrors that reflect the same old thing back to them day in and day out?

As we dare to speak about religion with people outside our convictions, inevitably the conversation will delve into matters that we feel passionately about. Our answers to these questions flow out of our faith, out of philosophical traditions, teachings, and consciences. After all we have been raised to experience our ideological convictions in a specific room, which arranged the furniture around a specific worldview. The ASR unflinchingly engages the great mysteries of life. Some of those questions are: Should we love all people or just those like us? Do Christians, Muslims, and Jews believe in the same God? How are monotheisms similar and different? What about traditions that hold to more than one god or goddess? What are holy books? Why do we consider some people holy or honorable and others not?

The hallway is a safe place for serious conversations so long as we do not seek to force others, either by physical or mental coercion, to move into our rooms against their wills. If we seek to pressure or bully others, our dialogue will break down and people will certainly flee into their apartments, bolting the doors behind them against our religiously or philosophically motivated aggressions. This is basic civility: we allow ourselves our convictions. The ASR does not allow jargoned cruelty to carry the day. Curiosity, however, usually wins out in the end and nearly all who find themselves in the hall will appreciate such engagement. In fact, many will delight in it.

If speaking about religion is to have any sense of harmony, I would argue it needs to celebrate diversity. Allow me another example to make this point. In a choir there is need of sopranos, conductors, altos, musicians, tenors, tech people, basses, instrumentalists, and an audience at the least, if it is to have any hope of offering a melodious concert. The singers come together not by all singing the same pitches and rhythms, by only just listening to one person while others sit around, or by having one group sing all the time. We are all different; the wonder of the world is not revealed in the elimination of difference, but when it is celebrated by means of a experience in which all participate. Only when individuals know and play their parts can we say that a performance is what it should be.

The best classrooms, which are focused upon the ASR, are not one's where the professor or expert tells everyone else what to think. That would be like forcing everyone to sing the same notes and rhythm and would deny the reality that people are different. Indeed, to do so would reduce the experience to a monosyllabic monotony.

Leonard Swidler (a professor of Catholic thought and interreligious dialogue) and Paul Moizes (a professor of religious studies at Rosemont College) have suggested that dialogue happens on a continuum along four main points. On one extreme there is "destructive dialogue"—conversation that happens in a polarized way as people seek to force their own ideas on others. Next there is "disinterested dialogue"—discourse where people tolerate each other, but that's about as far as it goes. In this case, prejudices and hatred easily remain below the surface, even if people are willing to have conversation. "Dialogical dialogue" is where parties actually listen to each other and learn something in the process; this is the beginning of compassionate listening and understanding. Finally, there is "deep dialogue," a place where people can be transformed by conversations to seek the mutual benefit of all involved.[4] The ASR strives for "deep dialogue," but in reality, this happens less frequently than dialogical dialogue. Both dialogical and deep dialogue require a safe space, a safe hallway people can get into. When deep dialogue happens, most know it, and people walk away from the conversation moved or changed in some way.

How can deep dialogue happen? Swidler and Moizes offer ten rules that help bring about these important types of conversations.

> Rule 1: The primary purpose of dialogue is to learn—that is, to change and grow in the perception and understanding of reality, and then to act accordingly.
>
> Rule 2: Interreligious and interideological dialogue must be a two-sided equal engagement.
>
> Rule 3: Everyone must come to dialogue with as much honesty and sincerity as they can muster; the more they muster, the deeper the dialogue will go.

---

4. Swidler, *Religion in an Age of Global Dialogue*, 156.

Rule 4: Interreligious and interideological dialogue must not compare our ideals with other's practices. Compare ideals to ideals, practices to practices. Compare your best to their best, not the worst actions of a random few to your highest ideals.

Rule 5: Participants need to define themselves for others, not have others define them.

Rule 6: Dialogue requires setting aside hard-and-fast assumptions about points of disagreement.

Rule 7: Dialogue only can take place between equals.

Rule 8: Dialogue only can take place with mutual trust.

Rule 9: Interfaith and interideological dialogue requires self-critical reflection about our own traditions and beliefs; this means seeing the worst of our history as well as the best.

Rule 10: Participants seek to grasp other religions or ideologies with an empathetic imagination, "from within" not just with the judgmental head "from without."[5]

The ASR promotes all these rules. They are not as easy as they may appear. At times comments that compare the best of our own tradition to the worst actions of a few random individuals in another emerge all too easily in speaking about religion. I have heard people say, "Muslims destroyed the World Trade Center. Therefore, all Muslims are terrorists." However, if a few radicals, who claimed to be Muslim, perpetrated this action, how can we blame the whole for the part? But such an opinion is fairly widespread.

Muslim leaders have consistently condemned the 9/11 attacks, but such voices are ignored. One student said, "I've never heard of Muslims condemning the attack." I made him, and my class, read an interfaith document spearheaded by Muslims and other religious leaders, called, "A Common Word." It not only strongly denounced the terrorist actions of 9/11 but all such deeds in the name of religion or otherwise. "A Common Word" likewise strongly endorses compassionate interfaith cooperation and dialogue.[6] My student was a bit sheepish and said, "I guess I have to do research before I make such broad claims." Indeed.

When I ask students to compare the worst of their tradition to the above 9/11 example, after some hesitation, they can easily come up with

---

5. Swidler, *Religion in an Age of Global Dialogue*, 1; these are paraphrased.
6. "A Common Word" at https://www.acommonword.com/.

similar instances. Christianity, for example, has groups who claim to be Christian and have carried out terrorist acts. White supremacists and Neo-Nazi movements in the USA and around the world regularly claim to represent Christianity as they justify their hate and violence against African Americans, Jews, immigrants, and others.[7] Every religious tradition can find such extremists in their midst.

Using the previous logic about Muslims, a similar argument could be made the opposite way, "Since Christian white supremacist factions are racist, all Christians are racist." When I bring this up, my students react strongly and claim that such racist groups don't deserve to be called "Christian." Then in the "Aha!" moment they are able to realize the same claim about Muslim terrorists is also true, namely they aren't Muslims, but people who use those claims to perpetrate violence. Comparing our best to the best of others or their worst to our worst can expose our own prejudices, which often are ignored.

Allow me another example to further illustrate the above important point from a slightly different angle. If you travel to Dachau, Auschwitz, or other former Nazi concentration camps, you will often see historical posters hanging therein that show that the Nazis not only put yellow stars of David on all the Jews to mark them as "other" and "lesser," but they also forced many other symbols on people to distinguish them from what Hitler called the "Aryan master race." They assigned pink triangles to gay people and other colored triangles were pinned on political prisoners (especially those who opposed the Nazi party), pacifists, people accused of being prostitutes, Jehovah's witnesses, gypsies, people with mental health issues or disabilities, and many more. These "badges of shame," as the Nazis referred to them, are reminders of how often societies promote an ideology in order to promote fear, hate, violence, and even genocide.

Sometimes when we speak of religion, we mentally pin colored badges of shame onto others. We do this when we denigrate others by insisting on our superiority and by driving out diversity for the sake of conformity. There has never been a society that employed "badges of shame" that has not also used fear, hatred, and violence to oppress minorities. What is remarkable is how often countries return to such tactics, especially in times of hardship, regularly. Such attitudes are dangerous, and every compassionate religious and philosophical tradition over the ages has spoken out and actively worked against them; when they have they also have become the

---

7. Michael Luo, "American Christianity's White Supremacy Problem."

object of their ire. Such movements of fear want to eliminate the hallway, tear down the house, and force everyone into an ideological bunker, where the haves rule and the have nots serve at their whim.

The ASR strives for a spirit of understanding while celebrating diversity. Real compassionate insights and deeds of lovingkindness to benefit the common good can flow from such encounters when we look beyond ourselves to truly see others. A central hallmark of the ASR is that it creates and honors the safe place, the hallway of compassionate, convicted, and civil dialogue, where enlightenment occurs amid humility, humor, and humanitarian concern for all.

5

Healthy Dialogue

The Uncommon Decency of Compassionate Convicted Civility

"This disdain [the idea of feeling religiously superior
to others] is a real spiritual disease.
It lies in the conflict between truth and love."

—Helmut Thielicke (d. 1986) *A Little Exercise for Young Theologians*

"The point is one that speaks to us all:
the moment we human beings grasp God with jealousy
and possessiveness, we lose hold of God.
One might add that the religious point here
is quite the opposite of God's jealousy . . .;
it is God's infinite capacity to love
and the problem of human jealousy."

—Diana L. Eck (b. 1945) *Encountering God*

Speaking of Religion . . .

The compassionate safe space of the ASR requires empathy and vulnerability. Whenever we speak of religion, there is always a fear of rejection or ridicule by others, but when humility creates an air of openness, then beautiful, even life-changing compassionate, convicted, and civil conversations can occur.

Krista Tippett on her National Public Radio show called "Civil Conversations" makes the observation that in the past many used to think that "tolerance" was the way people should treat each other. Tolerance, however, notes Tippett, is not good enough, because it often simply means putting up with others, while deep-seeded disdain remains. Tolerance does not call for engagement in the hallway, but merely requires that people not make too much eye contact or bump into each other while they pass by each other in the hall. Simple tolerance can never create a meaningful compassionate interest in others. The world doesn't need tolerance, argues Tippett, it needs heartfelt, thoughtful, and meaningful conversation that leads to kindness. The ASR strives for such discourse.[1]

The ASR in recent years has had some remarkable pioneers who have sought to move the discipline beyond just learning information in order to pass a test, to true transformational encounters. An example of an educator, activist, author, and popular speaker who has made a profound difference in the world of the ASR is Eboo Patel.[2] His book, *Acts of Faith: The Story of an American Muslim, the Struggle for the Soul of a Generation,* outlines how he came to be a community leader and activist who seeks to bring people together despite wildly diverse religious and social backgrounds. His method? Interfaith dialogue.

Patel recognized that, social movements for positive change historically had often developed among youth on college campuses. He established the Interfaith Youth Corp (IFYC) to train and send into communities honest and enthusiastic young leaders to promote interfaith cooperation.[3] The IFYC mission puts it this way, "We believe that a less divided and more pluralistic future requires new leaders at its core. When they leave college equipped with the vision, knowledge, and skills to positively engage

---

1. Krista Tippett at http://www.civilconversationsproject.org/.
2. Patel holds a doctorate in sociology of religion from Oxford University, where he studied as a Rhodes scholar.
3. Patel, *Acts of Faith,* 61–74.

difference, our religiously diverse democracy can and will flourish."[4] A religiously pluralistic society, for IFYC, has three key characteristics:

> **Respect for Identities**—where people have the right to form their own religious or non-religious worldviews, express them freely, and expect some reasonable accommodations to live out their convictions. To respect someone else's worldview doesn't require you to agree with it or to accept it.
>
> **Mutually Inspiring Relationships**—where there are conversations, activities, civic association, and friendly contact between people who orient around religion differently. Areas of both commonality and difference are recognized, but there is always some essential concern for the other's wellbeing.
>
> **Commitment to the Common Good**—where different people share common values, even despite theological disagreements, and support the things people generally agree that we have a collective interest to uphold. Think safe communities, good schools, defeating poverty, access to healthcare, and addressing climate change.[5]

Along with the aforementioned work, Patel's other works—*Sacred Ground: Pluralism, Prejudice, and the Promise of America* and *Out of Many Faiths*—are often used as introductory texts in courses on the ASR. They offer useful bridge-building tools and offer access to training programs, seminars, written resources, and grants so that people may be empowered to find ways beyond the current gridlock of ideological wall building. For IFYC, this is a way of fulfilling the best of our destiny as a society. Speaking specifically about the USA their website concludes, "In the end, interfaith cooperation is a way of moving America closer to its ideals, but it is also an act of citizenship. When you work to bring people into relationships, even when forging that link is difficult, you actively strengthen the bonds that hold our society together. In divided times, that citizenship is more important than ever."[6]

Patel's work is indebted to the pioneering scholarship of Diana Eck, a professor of religious studies at Harvard University.[7] In the early 1990s

---

4. https://ifyc.org/mission.

5. https://ifyc.org/interfaith.

6. https://ifyc.org/interfaith.

7. Eck is also the Professor of Comparative Religion and Indian Studies, the Frederic Wertham Professor of Law and Psychiatry in Society, and a faculty member at Harvard Divinity School.

Eck says that she felt "the very ground beneath my feet as a teacher and a scholar begin to shift."[8] She was surprised to discover that diversity in her classrooms included "Muslims from Providence, Hindus from Baltimore, Sikhs from Chicago, Jains from New Jersey" and others. Eck notes, "[This] signaled to me the emergence in America of a new cultural and religious reality about which I knew next to nothing."[9] As a result she began to develop new ways of exploring difference in and outside the classroom by promoting what she called "pluralism."

Put simply, Eck's definition of pluralism is as follows:

> Pluralism is not diversity alone, but the *energetic engagement with diversity*. Pluralism is not just tolerance, but the *active seeking of understanding across lines of difference*. Pluralism is not relativism, but the *encounter of commitments*. Pluralism is *based on dialogue*. The language of pluralism is that of dialogue and encounter, give and take, criticism and self-criticism. Dialogue means both speaking and listening; it reveals both common understandings and real differences.[10]

For Eck this means that "truth is not the exclusive or inclusive possession of any one tradition or community. Therefore, the diversity of communities, traditions, understandings of truth, and visions of God is not an obstacle for us to overcome, but an opportunity for our energetic engagement and dialogue with one another."[11] Eck firmly believes that this sort of dialogue is not some sort of wishy-washy everything-goes relativism, or a minimizing or homogenization of differences. Rather it requires that people cling to their own convictions with passion as they engage others so there might be a "give-and-take of mutual discovery, understanding, and indeed, transformation."[12]

Eck distinguishes pluralism from exclusivism and inclusivism as other ways that people deal with religious difference. Religious exclusivism is defined as the belief that there is only one exclusive ultimate truth, or only one means or way of salvation or believing. Eck says an exclusivist would argue, "Our own community, our tradition, and our understanding of reality, our

---

8. Eck, "Pluralism Project."

9. Eck, "Pluralism Project." Also see Eck, *A New Religious America*.

10. Eck, "Pluralism Project." Also see Eck, *Encountering God*. Author's emphasis in the quote.

11. Eck, *Encountering God*, 170.

12. Eck, *Encountering God*, 170.

encounter with God, is the one and only truth, excluding all others."[13] Douglass Pratt[14] puts it this way, "Exclusivism is more than simply a conviction about the transformative power of the particular vision one has; it is a conviction about its finality and its absolute priority over competing views."[15] When people hold to this position, it becomes difficult, as has been pointed out in previous chapters, to foster a healthy environment when speaking about religion. Exclusivists, when they do venture into the hallway, have a hard time talking about anything else besides encouraging people to come move into and live with them in their ideological rooms.

Inclusivism, on the other hand, Eck argues is the view that says there are "many communities, traditions, and truths, but our own way of seeing things is the culmination of the others, superior to the others, or at least wide enough to include the others under our universal canopy and in our own terms." Eck explains it this way: if the exclusivists believe that their God doesn't listen to others, the inclusivist would say that God is "indeed listening, but it is our God as *we* understand God who does the listening." Whereas the pluralist would say, "'Our God' is listening, but God is not ours, God is our way of speaking of a Reality that cannot be encompassed by any one religious tradition, including our own."[16]

Pluralism for Eck allows room for people to cling to what their consciences compel them to believe without minimizing anyone else's conscience. She admits this is a difficult tension for people to hold, because we all believe we are right. Eck, however, also cautions, "While we speak of exclusivist, inclusivist, and pluralist as if they were entirely different groups of people, let us remember that these ways of thinking about diversity may well be a part of the ongoing dialogue within ourselves."[17] Sometimes we move back and forth between convictions; this is especially evident when we start speaking about religion with people outside of our tradition.

Eck holds that today the exclusivist position in the USA is the most loudly expressed, but that inclusivism is the most popular position.

---

13. Eck, *Encountering God*, 170.

14. Pratt is the Professor of Studies in Religion at the University of Waikato, New Zealand, and Adjunct Professor of Theology and Interreligious Studies at the University of Bern, Switzerland. He is an associate of the Centre for the Study of Religion and Politics at the University of St Andrews, Scotland, and the New Zealand Associate, UNESCO Chair in Interreligious and Intercultural Relations Asia—Pacific.

15. Pratt, "Exclusivism and Exclusivity," 296.

16. Eck, *Encountering God*, 170.

17. Eck, *Encountering God*, 170.

Speaking of Religion . . .

Inclusivist Christians, argues Eck, believe that the "evangelical message of Christianity is not exclusive. . . . No indeed—the invitation is open, and the tent of Christ is wide enough for all." For inclusivist Christians, argues Eck, "other religious traditions are not so much evil or wrong-headed as incomplete, needing the fulfillment of Christ."[18] C. S. Lewis expressed inclusivist tendencies when he said, "I think that every prayer which is sincerely made even to a false god . . . is accepted by the true God and that Christ saves many who do not think they know him."[19] But Eck also notes, "While [inclusivism] often preserves the integrity of [its] own self-understanding, inclusivism often dodges the question of real difference by reducing everything finally to [its] own terms."[20]

Eck concludes that every religious or ideological conviction includes these three positions. Not only Christians, but Muslims, Jews, Hindus, and others, even atheists, need to make sense of how they will apply their convictions to people who hold different views. We all must choose how we will behave in the hallway when speaking of religion. Knowing where we stand with regard to these three convictions of exclusivism, inclusivism, and pluralism can help move us to deep dialogue.

The noted poet Elizabeth Alexander, who read her famous poem "Praise Song for a Day" at President Obama's inauguration, has argued that "Without a loving curiosity of the other we will never be able to create a good society."[21] The ASR promotes such curiosity. In the hallway of understanding, people can begin to set aside stereotypes and false assumptions and start to see people as real flesh and blood human beings, who have the same hopes and desires for lasting happiness.

Allow me a personal example to expand on the above ideas. Back in 2007, my son, Jeremiah, who is a documentary filmmaker, traveled to Pakistan to make a documentary about Allama Muhammad Iqbal, entitled *Message from the East*. Iqbal was a key voice in the formation of the nation of Pakistan, a highly revered poet, a religious leader, and one of the most important Muslim thinkers of the modern era.

I went along primarily to help with logistics and as a consultant on the project. I never dreamed how much my life would be changed. As a college

---

18. Eck, *Encountering God*, 179.
19. Lewis, *Letters*, 247; cf. Eck, *Encountering God*, 179.
20. Eck, *Encountering God*, 184.
21. For more see http://www.elizabethalexander.net/front-page-1 and https://onbeing.org/programs/desire-know-elizabeth-alexander-2/.

professor engaged in international travel—I have been involved in taking students abroad to Europe, Turkey, and Egypt for over twenty years—I had experienced diversity and worked with students to think about their experiences with other cultures and religions in a constructive pluralistic manner. I had thought I was comfortable with being a minority in another land, but in Pakistan I was forced into the darkest corner of the basement of my own prejudices. I had never been in a country of such poverty nor had I ever been so fully removed from my comfortable western cultural context.

On one Friday afternoon, we went to the magnificent ancient Wasir Kahn Mosque in the heart of the old city of Lahore for Jumu'ah (Friday) prayers. My son and his film crew were soon set up in the towering minarets filming the crowd below, but the stairways were narrow, and space was limited, so I was forced to stay in the main worship area as the prayers commenced. Suddenly, with a bit of a shock, I realized that in a short while there would be thousands of Muslims in the splendid square for prayers and I was, as far as I knew, going to be the only American and Christian there. I felt like I had a sign on my back that said, "Outsider! Stranger! I don't belong here!" I am loathed to admit that a fear welled up within me. I was puzzled by the emotion and wondered why? I supposed that it was because I was the "other" in this strange land. I had grown up with strong exclusivist views of religion, and some residue of that bubbled up to the surface. If my view of the world was right, then theirs must be wrong, and I was surrounded. I know it doesn't sound rational, but that's the way of emotions sometimes. My pluralist engagements with Muslims now receded into some sort of irrational fear.

On my previous trips with students, we had always been accompanied by guides, who helped us to negotiate difference. Here I was suddenly alone: I didn't speak the language or know what was culturally appropriate in this context. It is embarrassing to confess, but I literally tried to hide in the back of the courtyard off to one side, hoping no one would notice me. I had thought of leaving, but I did not think hanging around the outside of the mosque was any better, so I tried to fade into the stonework.

The stereotypes and prejudices that lurked within me, planted there by family, friends, media, and my American culture, showed themselves to me. If I am honest, I am not sure that I even knew they were there until I was confronted with this situation. These insidious anxieties had been firmly rooted in some of the most clandestine places within my soul and now they burst forth. Muslims streamed into the mosque, gathered in front of me in the massive courtyard in a country that a *Newsweek* magazine cover recently had called, "The most dangerous country in the world."[22] People gave me strange stares that seemed to shout, "What are *you* doing here?" Although I now realize that was just my own insecurities speaking.

Unexpectedly I noticed an elderly man staring at me with curiosity from across the courtyard. I turned away quickly, nervously trying to avoid his gaze, but undeterred he strode over to me. Close up, he looked as if he was about seventy years old, but his youthful eyes and remarkable energy made me unsure of this assessment. When it became clear I could not escape him, I said, "*As-salamu alaykum*" (that is, "Peace be upon you"). He said, "*Wa 'alaykumu s-salam*" (". . . and peace also be with you"). Sizing me up, he smiled and asked in perfect English if he could help me. How did he know I spoke English? In the previous days I had been mistaken for German or Dutch, but he had no hesitation. I back peddled. "No, thank you. I'm fine." I quickly explained to him that I was only there because my son and his film crew were shooting a film. I pointed at the minaret where he could see the cameras poking out the windows.

He smiled broadly and asked, "Brother, are you a Muslim?" My heart sank. I paused. In my mind, I wondered if it was it safe to say, "No." Surely if I tried deception, I'd be found out. Besides I didn't want to do that. Some illogical fear wondered if I wasn't supposed to be there; even though I knew better—I had taken students to Jumu'ah prayers before in many countries. Maybe I had broken some cultural norm for Pakistan that I was unaware of. Possibly I had offended him and others with my presence? Would he kick me out of the mosque? Then what? A thousand thoughts ran through my head in an instant. But notice, my first suppositions were to assume the worst. So, unable to find an evasive answer, I told him the truth, "No, I'm a Christian." After a brief conversation, I even admitted that I was a pastor, and a professor of religion at a Christian College. Why? I have no idea, it just tumbled out.

What happened next was a wonder. First, he merely smiled warmly at me with a genuine compassion that I could sense. He did not try to convince me of the superiority of Islam then or later. He just cared for me and seeing my ill-at-ease demeanor, he sought to comfort me. Even now as I write these words, I see his wrinkled face, compassionate grin, and gently extended hands nearly as clearly as when it happened. Then he embraced me.

---

22. *Newsweek*, October 31, 2007.

I was thunderstruck. I hugged his frail body, afraid of breaking something. He coughed roughly from what sounded like an advanced smoker's cough.

He said, "Brother, you are a believer, and I am a believer. Come pray with me. You as a Christian and I as a Muslim." I hesitated, pondering. "Was this allowed?" Do Muslim customs or does my own faith permit such a thing? While he offered a sincere pluralistic encounter, as Eck would define it, I hesitated. Even though I am a professor of religion who has studied Islam for decades, as we spoke, my mind went blank, overridden by some dark fears from a day gone by. In a moment that I cannot explain other than to say that I seemed to observe the whole event from the outside of myself, I heard myself say to him, "I'd like that." He had won me over. I stepped into an experience that was outside of tradition or teaching, into a place made possible by true compassion.

Now, in order to pray in a mosque, one must go through a ritual washing. He immediately, politely, but firmly dragged me over to the fountains and he taught me what to do. I did it poorly, but he was a patient with me, at times asking me to try some aspect of it again with more attention to detail. Once satisfied, he led me off to pray. Together we knelt side-by-side. For him, and apparently all those around me, it mattered not a bit that I was Christian in the midst of Muslims. Together we lifted our voices to the heavens as I imitated the bowing and standing of those around me: I wanted to fit in and not draw too much attention to myself. Now I am sure there are many in his and my tradition who would see this as some sort of betrayal at best and heretical at worst. Such views well up from exclusivist and inclusivist convictions. But my experience suggested to me quite the opposite. For me, it was a moment of grace. A time when we together sought our common humanness.

I had two strong emotions that came to me later that day. Shame that I had somehow absorbed the stereotypes offered to me in my society and joy in having found a brother in a place I had feared was hostile to me. My country and members among my own religious tradition often see Muslims as enemies, and at that time it was also impossible for me to set those feelings completely aside. But now, I find it harder not to see how a world where people pray together to their God or work together for humanity is not a much more civil world. In my new friend, who called me brother, I saw all Muslims anew. In this strangely anxiety-filled experience, in the caring curiosity of a kind gnarled old Muslim man named Muhammad, I was transformed.

Speaking of Religion . . .

After the prayers were over, he told me that he was a teacher and that he had brought his forty or so students there for their devotions. He wanted me to meet them. He bustled off and gathered them together. He told me that I was going to be their class for the afternoon. He wanted them to get to know me. We talked for quite some time. They asked questions. What did I think of their mosque? Of Pakistan? What was it like where I lived? Do I have kids or a dog? I remember some of the younger students (the lot of them probably ranged in age from ten to eighteen) placing their hands on my sleeves. They did so, I think, to see if a Christian from halfway around the world and an American whose politicians often spoke quite ill of them, was really in fact standing in their mosque with them. At some point I wondered if they were as afraid of me, as I had been of them. Perhaps they too sought to reconcile being near to me because of things they had been taught. By the end of the day, despite my fears and apprehensions, my new friend, Muhammad, had become dear to me, and now when I hear of a bombing in Lahore I wonder if he or his students are safe. I pray for them regularly; I can't help myself.

It is important to remember, says Eck, that in such encounters we do not need to give up our cherished convictions. For example, I didn't need to stop being a Christian in the mosque. We simply need to embrace our differences and seek out common ground and stand on it. But this is still easier said than done. The key to creating relationships, sometimes surprising friendships, is simply to start seeing each other as fellow human beings. Often, this happens in the most unexpected moments and places of our lives, where we are forced to confront ourselves first, so we can truly be free to seek friendships that we may have once thought impossible.

Allow me a thought experiment to see if I can put you into my shoes in the mosque for a moment. Try to be honest and see yourself honestly for a moment. What do you actually feel when you read the following words?—read the next list slowly . . . stop after each word . . . and consider your emotions as you see the words . . . perhaps even write out your emotional response after the word on another piece of paper . . . ready?—abortion, Donald Trump, immigration, climate change, gun control, Barack Obama, universal health care, evolution, border wall, feminism, euthanasia, racism, LGBTQ+, creationism, Democrat, Republican. Which words did you react to most strongly? Were they the ideas you agreed with? Were they the ideas you disagree with? Why do you think that is the case? All of these words have become trigger buzzwords, ideas that sit like time bombs threatening to set us off when stepped upon in conversations. Notice that they are often tied to exclusivist views.

Do you think it is possible for you to sit down and have a genuinely compassionate, convicted, and civil conversation with somebody who holds views opposite to the one's you hold on the topic you reacted to most strongly?

Richard Mouw, an Evangelical Christian theologian and former president of Fuller Theological Seminary, a well-known religiously conservative school, wrote over twenty-five years ago a book entitled *Uncommon Decency: Christian Civility in an Uncivil World*, whose message is even more true today than when originally developed. Mouw insists that we need to find ways to be in civil relationships with people with whom we strongly disagree. He argues that being hateful in language or action is not a part of being Christian, or a good person, but rather Christians in particular must always act with love toward the other, even their worst enemies. Mouw points to Jesus words, "Love your enemy and pray for those who persecute you, so that you may be children of your Father in heaven" (Matthew 5:44) as his rationale. For Mouw this begins with how we speak to and about others. He believes people need to restore civility with kind language and loving actions, an "uncommon decency." In the ASR, such an attitude is necessary in order for fruitful dialogue to flourish.

An interesting strategy that Mouw uses to create understanding is to ask the following questions: "What is it about people like me that scares you?" And, "What is it about what you are advocating that worries me so much?" These questions get to the heart of fear and can open the door to deep dialogue. If you've never tried this, and few of us have, because we are more and more resistant to talking with people we disagree with, you will find that the risk is worth the effort. But it is not easy. Those who have good humor can, however, come to learn much from this method.[23]

Mouw also insightfully says that it is dangerous and one of the great tragedies of history that people define themselves by how they label and treat their enemies. Allow me to offer a few examples concerning Mouw's last point to clarify the contention. During the time of Hitler's Germany, the Nazis defined themselves by how they labelled and hated Jews and other enemies of the state. Nazis sought to develop a pure Aryan race of like-minded ideologues who hated the Jews, communists, homosexuals, people with contrary political views, people of color, Romani (also known

---

23. Cf. Krista Tippett at http://www.civilconversationsproject.org/.

as gypsies), and so forth. To define a society by what it hates means that the society then actively marginalizes those believed to be threats to the ideals of the state, in this case an unpolluted bloodline—which science and DNA research has shown to be completely bogus. The development of extermination camps ensued.

We must not forget that concentration camps have been a regular part of history. During WWII the USA incarcerated about 120,000 Japanese Americans based on a fear of their enemy in Japan.[24] The US did not do this with Germans or Italians living in the USA in response to Nazi and Italian fascism: why? While the USA certainly saw the Nazi's and fascism as a threat, German or Italian citizens were seen by political groups to be more assimilated into society and so were not perceived of as enemies per se. The bombing of Pearl Harbor by the Japanese was also a direct attack on USA soil; something the European fascists had not done at that point. Either way, racist attitudes and fear moved American politics to see the Japanese as the enemy and so they were rounded up in large numbers. Again, Mouw's point is that the marginalization of enemies allows for horrific injustices.

During the 1950s, many in the USA, especially those sympathetic to McCarthyism, decided that patriotism was determined by hating communists: many in the USSR expressed loyalty to the state by loathing American capitalism. The so-called "Cold War" emerged out of such attitudes. Both sides of the conflict spent vast fortunes on nuclear weapons and brought the world to the brink of nuclear destruction. Both developed massive armies out of a "just in case" fear that the other might do something first.[25] Both nations were defined by their hatred and therefore diverted much of their nations resources into developing weapons of mass destruction, rather than caring for those in need.

It is important for governments to keep their people safe, Mouw admits, but it is also very dangerous to define ourselves by making our enemies something they are not. Mouw's book was published shortly after the events of 9/11. He saw many in America defining patriotism as being suspicious and fearful of all Muslims. Turning enemies into demons allows patriots of a cause or nations to dehumanize others, therefore allowing

---

24. Wikipedia notes that the official WRA record from 1946 puts the number at 120,000 people. See *War Relocation Authority (1946). The Evacuated People: A Quantitative Study*, 8. This number does not include people held in other camps such as run by the DofJ or Army. Other sources may give numbers slightly more or less than 120,000." See https://en.wikipedia.org/wiki/Internment_of_Japanese_Americans#cite_note-howmany-5.

25. Mouw, *Uncommon Decency*, 47.

them and even governments to justify oppressive policies, violence, and even warfare. Mouw decries fear and hatred, pointing out that they are not Christian virtues, but rather vices that corrupt souls.[26] G. K. Chesterton sums up this idea when he says, "Idolatry is committed, not merely by setting up false gods, but also by setting up false devils . . . ."[27]

Martin Marty, an ELCA Lutheran theologian and historian, believes that what we need more than anything else today is "convicted civility," a concept Richard Mouw has also embraced. Marty has observed that a lot of people who have strong convictions are not often very civil; they believe so strongly in their own views that anyone who doesn't agree with them is an enemy to be crushed or converted. He notably adds that it is also true that a lot of people who are civil, lack strong convictions. The poet Yeats (d. 1939) in his poem "The Second Coming" has put it this way, "The best lack all conviction, while the worst are full of passionate intensity."[28] Rather than being one of these extremes, says Marty, we should honor a convicted civility and return to a place where people can disagree and still work for the common good amid difference.

The ASR is at its best when it also promotes compassionate, convicted, and civil conversation when speaking of religion that moves people and communities to protect its most vulnerable members, namely minorities, the oppressed, and the disenfranchised. The ASR is a unique opportunity to create people who are dedicated to what Martin Luther King Jr.. called a "beloved community,"[29] a society that does not ignore, fear, hate, or treat ill anyone because of religion, race, gender, or difference. Speaking of this community, King said, "The end is reconciliation; the end is redemption; the end is the creation of the Beloved Community. It is this type of spirit and this type of love that can transform opponents into friends. It is this type of understanding goodwill that will transform the deep gloom of the old age into the exuberant gladness of the new age." Dr. King even argues that this is a type of love that will bring about miracles in the hearts of humanity.[30]

---

26. Mouw, *Uncommon Decency*, 47.

27. Chesterton, *Illustrated London News*, September 11, 1909.

28. *Norton Anthology of Poetry*.

29. Also see Smith, *Search for the Beloved Community*.

30. Shelton, *Blacks and Whites in Christian America*. See also http://www.thekingcenter.org/king-philosophy#sub4; Harding, *Hope and History*; Harding, *The Inconvenient Hero*; Harding *There Is a River*.

Speaking of Religion . . .

The miracle Dr. King longed for was a transformation of what he called a balance of opposites. The characteristics of tough-mindedness and soft-heartedness, he suggested, are the way to face a hostile and divided world. He observed,

> Let us consider, first, the need for a tough mind, characterized by incisive thinking, real appraisal, and decisive judgment. The tough mind is sharp and penetrating, breaking through the crust of legends and myths and sifting the true from the false. The tough-minded individual is astute and discerning. He has a strong, austere quality that makes for firmness of purpose and solidness of commitments.[31]

The soul of the ASR is such compassionate critical thinking. Tough-mindedness is difficult to come by, however; as Dr. King noted, it is in fact rare. Rather he suggests, "There is an almost universal quest for easy answers and half-baked solutions. Nothing pains some people more than having to think."[32] The ASR and Dr. King note that when people are soft-minded, they are gullible and especially open to slogans and labels that simplify difficult issues such as religion and race in a way that breaks down community. Tough-mindedness and clear thought, however, opens people up to the reality that compassionate, convicted civility is possible, if people are able to see where their problems of fear, hatred, and violence stem from. Dr. King writes, "Few people have the toughness of mind to judge critically and to discern true from false, the fact from the fiction. Our minds are constantly being invaded by legions of half-truths, prejudices, and false facts."[33] Already fifty years ago, Dr. King strongly warned that there will always be those who declare that falsehood is truth, and they should not be believed. The problem today is that both sides claim the other side is doing this. We desperately need tough-minded critical thinking to help us through the insanity of false claims.

The ASR teaches people how to sort through the path of propaganda to discover a more compassionate road to follow—ways with firm steps on convicted consciences and civil highways leading to beloved community. Says Dr. King, "There is little hope for us until we become tough minded enough to break loose from the shackles of prejudice, half-truths, and downright ignorance." He concludes by suggesting that a nation that

---

31. Martin Luther King Jr., *Strength to Love*, 2.
32. Martin Luther King Jr., *Strength to Love*, 2–3.
33. Martin Luther King Jr., *Strength to Love*, 3.

produces soft-minded people "purchases its own spiritual death on an installment plan."[34] The ASR trains the minds not to be soft but rather shows how to exercise minds with truth and empathy so that the beloved community can be imagined.

Dr. King, however, does not feel tough-mindedness is enough. The second part of the balance of opposites deals with cultivation of a tender heart. Often, alongside soft-mindedness comes the cold, detached, and hard heart that leaves "one's life in the perpetual winter devoid of the warmth of spring and the gentle heat of summer," says Dr. King. Hard-hearted people are utilitarian and rarely capable of loving others outside of their own circle. The beloved community is not possible because for the hard-hearted it belongs only to people of one race, religion, or some other limiting factor. Says Dr. King, "The hardhearted individual never sees people as people, but rather as mere objects or as impersonal cogs in an ever-turning wheel." They are instruments, tools, and depersonalized utilities that the advantaged employ for their own profit at the expense of the tool they abuse.[35] As a result, without tenderheartedness, no matter how tough-minded people may be, there will be no progress toward a beloved community.

The ASR suggests that while tough-mindedness is able to dream of the beloved community, it is tender-heartedness that promotes a type of compassionate, convicted, and civil dialogue that can actually bring about real-life community engagement, which fosters a vision of others as beloved and not detestable. So how does the ASR after teaching tough-mindedness and tenderheartedness actually begin to build a beloved community? The answer begins with conscience.

---

34. Martin Luther King Jr., *Strength to Love*, 5.
35. Martin Luther King Jr., *Strength to Love*, 5–6.

6

Creating Conscience
Discovering Self

"To go against one's conscience is neither right nor safe."
—Martin Luther (d. 1546) *The Diet of Worms*

"There comes a time when one must take a position
that is neither safe, nor politic, nor popular,
but he must take it because conscience tells him it is right."
—Martin Luther King Jr.. (d. 1968) *A Testament of Hope*

"What is conscience?" "How are our consciences pricked so that they move us to act with moral integrity?" "Why do our consciences fail us from time to time?" When I ask people these questions, they tend to pause in bewilderment. Certainly, they have a basic sense of conscience, that there is an inner voice we listen to in order to make decisions, but beyond that, they have rarely thought about these concepts. Allow me here to offer one way of speaking about conscience and an historical example of how it played out in the life of one famous figure, both in a positive and negative manner. In this way, I hope to help you as a reader to come to your own conclusion about what conscience is and how it works.

Paul Tillich, a Lutheran Theologian (d. 1965), in his *Dynamics of Faith*, simply explains that "Faith is the state of being ultimately concerned." He acknowledges that we have many practical concerns in life, like food and shelter, but we also have spiritual or transcendent convictions, which make up our ultimate concerns in life. We believe in an ultimate concern, says Tillich, when we "totally surrender" to our deepest belief. Whether we know it or not, we have always such a concern, and our sense of identity and our purpose for living flows out of it.

Some, for example, may trust in patriotism as their ultimate concern and totally surrender their lives to a specific brand of government, such as conservative or liberal ideologies, or perhaps they will simply pursue the success of their chosen nation more broadly. They identify with certain descriptive labels—such as Republican, Democrat, Libertarian, Socialist, Communist, American, Chinese, Indonesian, South Sudanese, Russian, and so forth—thus revealing their commitments. Their lives are dependent upon attaining the aspirations of their party or national agenda over and against those who might oppose them. They make decisions based on conscience and whether a choice does or does not benefit their goals.[1]

Whatever we set up as an ultimate concern, becomes our "God" if it is a worthy concern, argues Tillich, or a "god" or idol, if it is not. What he means by this is that some ultimate concerns are compassionate, and others are destructive. He warns that when we rely on gods, our faith totally surrenders to that which cannot in the end offer us true happiness. It is still an act of faith—or if you prefer, belief—to put our supreme trust in something, for Tillich, but sometimes it is simply misguided, self-serving, and even cruel.

A worthy trust in God, as Tillich develops the idea, comes when one loves God, who in turn moves people to love others and the world. I would broaden this idea a bit and argue, that atheists and agnostics can place their hope in worthy concerns as well, in a way that is not tied to God per se. If one surrenders totally to some higher power other than the individual, like the good of community, humanity, and the world, so long as it is centered on compassion, then one's concerns are worthy. In this instance, however, the ultimate concern cannot be narrowed down to caring for just a part of humanity or the world, but it must embrace the whole of humankind and

1. Tillich, *Dynamics of Faith*, 1–35.

existence. One example that comes readily to mind, which supports this idea, is when people make global warning their ultimate concern: to care about the good of the planet is to care about the good of all, and this is truly worthy. No doubt some readers will be thinking at this point, "Global warming is a hoax based on false science." Despite evidence to the contrary, such people make a decision like this based on their own ultimate concern, but what is it? When I've pressed students on this point they may answer, "Global warming hurts businesses and thus people trying to make a living." If I press further, they argue that it hurts big business, which in turn hires people. Pressed further it becomes clear that their motivation for holding this position on global warming is their political beliefs, which in the USA aligns with some members of the Republican Party. Inevitably, some Republicans say they also share concerns about global warming and so there is divisions among their ranks. What creates that division? Their ultimate concern. There are divisions among Democrats, Libertarians, Socialists, etc., as well, but they too are explainable by looking at ultimate concerns.

A caution is warranted here. People who make their "view" of God an ultimate concern, can ignore the idea of compassion for all people, because their ultimate concern is to make others over in their image, ignoring the experiences and consciences of others. The same can be true of any ideology.

How do unworthy concerns work? If, for example, our ultimate concern is success—say in celebrity, power, or wealth—then we lead lives that chase after these goals; our purpose in life thus is defined by the demands of attaining a particular level of success in whatever way we feel gives our lives meaning. If I make money my chief end, then its accumulation becomes my paramount purpose in life. I may feel I need enough money to be seen as someone others can admire, for security, or to support a lifestyle of the rich and famous. As a result, when faced with a decision of pursuing a specific major in college or job, my ultimate concern directs my conscience toward picking a major or job that will provide the biggest paycheck or accolades.

As one student told me once, "I'm really not good with people, but I want to become a doctor, because I want to be able to afford a nice house, a great car, a big lake home, and all the toys that will make me happy—like boats, jet skis, and snow mobiles." There was no altruism about helping others in his vision, it was simply about the bottom line, about what he thought would make him happy—being able to buy the stuff of temporary happiness.

More famous examples of people who got caught up in unworthy pursuits are plentiful. What durable happiness did the magnificent fortune of Howard Hughes (d. 1976), the wealthiest man in the world during his lifetime, bring him? He died a recluse and if his aids that were with him in the end can be trusted, he left this world largely broken and unhappy.[2] Some of our greatest novels, such as *The Great Gatsby*, and movies, such as *Citizen Kane*, tell the same story: making success an ultimate concern hollows out souls and leaves us without happiness or love. Sadly, many people lack the imagination to dream of a more fulfilling path to happiness than what they can physically lay their hands on. Of course, we all know this, but knowing and doing are two different things. Some say they want to be doctors for all the right reasons, but in the end lose their way. It is much easier to rely on the tangible than to do the work of self-examination that will lead to a life of compassionate convictions.

It is true that some who become wealthy, famous, or powerful have found ways of using their notoriety for the good of humanity, and in so doing have found a more lasting peace. But observe, their joy is not in the fleeting peace of success, but in charity, which is always a transcendent concern. One young woman I had as a student became a very successful as a lawyer. About ten years later when I saw her, I asked her about her work. She told me that when the initial enthusiasm of her early hectic lifestyle wore thin, she tired of the day in and day out rigorous cutthroat routine. She said, "I abandoned that life for a new one." She started working as a legal advocate for abused women, many of whom were poor. She said, "My work, although technically the same, was completely different. Beside that I began to consider those closest to me. I take time for my own family, a luxury I did not dare to indulge in too much before for fear of being lesser than my harder-working colleagues. I don't help the wealthy now, but I help the desperate. At times I donate my time or wave my fees altogether. I'm happier because I believe what I'm doing matters. I don't make as much money, but my life is better. Today I can honestly say working for justice in order to give hope is its own reward." Notice that this woman of privilege found a new way of being and acting that developed out of an ultimate concern of giving.

Another a former student, who became a doctor, once wrote to me to tell me that the ASR had helped her consider her purpose in life. She said, "I love being a doctor, because I have a strong sense of satisfaction when I help

---

2. See, https://www.history.com/this-day-in-history/howard-hughes-dies.

people. My institution encourages me to see more patients, to make more money, but I've slowed down. I try to care for them as individuals. I do not rush them out of the office. I also donate more of my time to organizations like 'Doctor's without Borders' whenever I have the opportunity."

Faith, for Tillich, is an act of the whole personality that comes about in the dynamics of daily personal living. We make decisions and act in accordance with our ultimate concern in the hope that our sense of purpose will offer us lasting satisfaction. Our thoughts, feelings, and experiences not only help create but are shaped by our ultimate concern. Or as Tillich put it, the "faith through which we believe" is the "faith which is believed."[3]

The faith that is believed is the ground out of which conscience grows. Conscience determines how we will act in a given situation. Conscience based upon a worthy ultimate concern pursues noble goals; conscience based upon temporal, easy, and self-serving ultimate concerns pursue ignoble goals. But always conscience is rooted in our ultimate concern, suggests Tillich.[4]

It is important to note at this juncture that our life experiences move us to take up one ultimate concern over and against another. If we say that we do or do not believe in God, for example, we do so for particular reasons, which are born out of experiences that have moved and shaped our emotions and reason. Our consciences, born out of our ultimate concern, dictate what we hold to be true and false, honorable and dishonorable, and so we act accordingly.

C. S. Lewis, who lost his mother at an early age, even though he had prayed fervently to God to heal her, concluded that a belief in a benevolent deity was nonsensical. His prayers hadn't worked, he said, so in his view God either didn't exist or didn't care. Lewis believed that he had no other choice but to become an atheist. He spent a good deal of his life operating with this as his core conviction. His early writings clearly reflect his belief that religion was nothing more than "lies breathed through silver."[5] After suffering through a horrific life as a soldier in the abominable trenches of WWI, Lewis wrote a book-length poem entitled *Spirits in Bondage*. He heartily proclaimed at one point, "We have cursed You, our Master, ere we

---

3. Tillich, *Systematic Theology*, vol. 1, 214–36; Tillich, *Dynamics of Faith*, 1–5.
4. Tillich, *Dynamics of Faith*, 102.
5. McGrath, *C.S. Lewis*, 20.

die, for all our hopes in endless ruin lie. We believe good is dead, and so, we curse You, God on high."[6]

Slowly over time, however, after numerous encounters with what Lewis called "Joy," he became convinced that there must be a benevolent God. Lewis would say that he was dragged "kicking, struggling, resentful, and with darting eyes" looking in every direction for a "chance to escape" into believing in a divinity. Slowly and reluctantly, Lewis changed. He did not do so because he wanted to but because he could not help himself, because of his life experiences.[7]

At the same time, Lewis's purpose in life shifted dramatically. He was a scholar and writer. As noted above, he wrote as an atheist when he was one, and later became one of the most popular Christian authors of the twentieth century. The sharp contrast between before and after can be explained by how he experienced the world through his ultimate concern, which had been born out of everyday moments of pain and hope. His conscience forced Lewis to write different types of books at different stages in his life. He literally could do no other.

Take a moment, if you will, and reflect on the idea of how traumatic life-events often profoundly shape our convictions. What tragedies have shaped you? How have they changed you? What is your ultimate concern that has grown out of these events? How has this concern shaped your conscience and the way you've acted and continue to act? How has suffering shaped your sense of self and purpose in life? Ask the same questions but this time from the perspective of moments of joy in your life.

The ASR unflinchingly examines how great authors in the past and anyone we engage in the present have discovered meaning and purpose in life. Often when we speak of religion, our convictions flow up from places of great anguish. That's one reason why it is so difficult to be criticized for what we believe: it literally feels like an attack on *who we are*. And indeed, in many ways it *is*. Likewise, when speaking about religion, it important to hear the stories that lie behind the convictions of others before we judge them. Without a compassionate curiosity in the other, in how their ultimate concern was born, we will never be able to see who others really are. Such myopic vision on our part becomes blindness, not because we *cannot* see, but because we *refuse to* by closing our eyes to truth.

---

6. Lewis, *Spirits in Bondage*, 20.
7. Lewis, *Surprised by Joy*, 23–24, 279.

Speaking of Religion . . .

How does the interplay of our ultimate concerns and conscience set us on a path worthy of traveling? First, there is no one example that can fully explain the remarkable complexity of conscience or the idea of the ultimate concern. Nevertheless, by looking at an historical example, I do believe we can gain some insight into how conscience may develop and work properly or go astray.

NOTE WELL: the following example is not meant to favor Lutheranism over Roman Catholicism or Christianity over atheism, but it is merely an illustration of how conscience developed in the person of Martin Luther (d. 1564). I believe there are some recognizable stages in the development of Luther's conscience. Not everyone goes through all of these stages, nor will people necessarily resonate with Luther. I merely wish to point out that Luther made some interesting choices and some dreadful mistakes of conscience, which when examined can help us understand conscience in our own lives a bit better. My goal here is simply to provide an illustration that can be instructive to help the reader draw their own conclusions of conscience, how it functions, and why it is important.

Many historians have noted that Martin Luther's appeal to conscience in 1521 was an historic event. In that year, Luther stood before the Holy Roman Emperor, Charles V at the Diet of Worms, which demanded that Luther recant his writings. Luther refused. For the past four years Luther had spoken out against what he called the evil practices of selling indulgences—the selling of certificates of assurance that claimed that the souls of dead loved ones were granted freedom from purgatory in exchange for money donated to the church on their behalf. Luther told the emperor that unless he was shown by scripture and pure reason the error of his beliefs, he could not go against his conscience. To do so, he argued, "was neither right nor safe." However, if he was convinced by scripture and pure reason that he was wrong, Luther said he would be the first to cast his books into the fire.[8] How did it come to this?

Luther was raised in the traditions and teachings of the Roman Catholic Church. His mother, Margarethe, known as Hannah to her family, was a very devout Catholic. His father, Hans, was also Catholic, but by most accounts he was much less pious than his wife. Martin perceived of himself to be a loyal son of the church. Hans, an ambitious and successful copper miner, gave his bright son an excellent education, something that few

---

8. Loewenich, *Martin Luther*, 195.

Creating Conscience

others of his day could afford. Eventually, Luther went off to the university so that he could make something of himself and do his father proud.[9]

Luther loved music, friends, beer, and a life of a certain amount of frivolity: in this he was a very ordinary youth. He was a gifted and serious student and so he chose a career path, in part due to pressures from his father, that would eventually afford him wealth that would provide him with a comfortable life. He studied to be a lawyer, one of the most profitable professions of his day. He excelled in his studies, but unexpectedly, a crisis befell him.[10]

One day, after a visit with his family, Luther was on his way back to his university in Erfurt. A fierce thunderstorm broke out and lightening crashed about him. Luther feared for his life. Convinced that God had caused the thunderstorm, because God was angry with him, Luther cried out to the mother of the Blessed Virgin Mary, the patron saint of travelers in trouble, "Saint Anne! Saint Anne! Spare me and I will become a monk."[11] In that plea to the heavens, he threw away a promising lucrative public legal career for a life of poverty, solitude, and prayer in a monastery.[12]

Although rarely so dramatic or direct, many of us at some point in our lives have life-defining moments. They may be, metaphorically speaking, lightning-bolt experiences: the loss of a loved one, personal injury or illness, emotional or psychological despair, issues with addiction, relationship troubles, economic trials, a stroke of good fortune, or a moment of overwhelming joy. Such moments shape our lives, often permanently. Just as importantly they profoundly affect the way we think and act in the world. They surely shape our ultimate concern, and we may even decide our life-path based upon them.

Sometimes such life-altering events, when explained to someone else, may be dismissed as insignificant, foolish, or insane. Many, especially his father, Hans Luther, dismissed Luther's thunderstorm experience as nothing more than an unstable emotional response to an unlucky chance tempest upon a muddy road. What really matters, however, is not the event itself, but the perception of what happened. The perceived reality, no matter how mundane, defines the self, shapes meaning, and creates a purpose in life. For Luther, he saw himself as lacking God's good will, he wanted to

---

9. Oberman, *Luther*, 90.
10. Oberman, *Luther*, 91–92.
11. Loewenich, *Martin Luther*, 15–16.
12. Oberman, *Luther*, 125.

Speaking of Religion . . .

change that, so he went off to the monastery. In many instances, it is not one event, but a series of gradual experiences that forms us. But in any case, our ultimate concern, as Tillich puts it, is born again and we cannot go back to being the person we once were. Luther gave up his merry life and pursuit of wealth focused on comfort for the austerity of monastic living directed at God.

Luther certainly could have reasoned his way out of his rash vow, but he did not. True to his oath, two weeks later, he found himself at the doorstep of the local Augustinian Abbey in Erfurt asking for entrance. Luther, reflecting on the experience, states simply that he fled to monastery to appease an angry God.[13] Later in life, when he less thunderstruck, Luther was less clear about his decision. Luther described the event to his friend Melanchthon, "I am uncertain with what kind of an attitude I took my vow [to St. Anne and God]. I was more overpowered than drawn. God wanted it this way. I am afraid that I, too, may have taken my vow in an impious and sacrilegious way."[14] By this he meant that he ran off to the monastery at least in part with a joyless and involuntary heart, hoping he would turn aside God's wrath. What is clear is that Luther believed that he had no choice in the matter. Total surrender, nothing else would put all to right.

In Luther's day, the most common way to get square with God was to embrace the vows of poverty, chastity, and obedience—which life as a friar of the Augustinian Order demanded—and receding into the interior world of the cloister. Luther noted, "I did not become a monk of my own free will and desire, still less to gain any gratification of the flesh, but . . . I was walled up in my terror and the agony of sudden death and was forced by necessity to take the vow."[15] Despite knowing he was motivated by the "terror and agony of sudden death," Luther's conscience would not allow him to go back on his word. His conscience moved him to a purpose, to love God so that God would return the favor.

I've had several students who have mirrored Luther's life experience on this point in some way: a turning from one path to another because some life-event has compelled them, leaving them with no other choice. One student told me that she was devastated by the diagnosis of her mother's breast cancer. She shifted away from her English literature major to

---

13. Lohse, *Martin Luther*, 22–23; Loewenich, *Martin Luther*, 56.
14. WABr 2:238; LW 48:300–301; Loewenich, *Martin Luther*, 56.
15. WA 8:513, LW 48:332; Loewenich, *Martin Luther*, 55.

being pre-Med, and eventually went into the field of oncology in order to help her mother and others.

Another pupil told me that he wanted to go into politics because his family, who had been elected to important political offices in his home state, had been viciously maligned. As he told the story, despite their best efforts to work for the people, they had been ridiculed by both political extremes. The youth believed in the good work of his family and did not want the cruelty of politics to win out. He went on to champion their cause.

One woman switched her major to psychology with the hope to go into addiction counseling, because she fortunately had emerged from her own alcohol and drug dependence. She not only needed to find ways to keep herself sober, but she believed that she could help others do the same.

Many years ago, I met an executive from a large automotive company, who got fed up with spending years in the hectic world of the automotive industry. He left his incredibly lucrative career after a series of frustrations and health issues and went off to the seminary to become a pastor, despite being in his mid-fifties. He said it wasn't any one thing that drove him to this radical change, but a lifetime of soul-sucking work. He told me, "I want to end my working life doing something meaningful; I want to give back. I don't know why I didn't leave sooner. Now that I'm out of that world, I see what it was doing to me. Now I'm free."

After Luther decided to join the monastery, says Martin Brecht, "(Luther's) father 'went crazy' and acted like a fool. He wrote his son a letter . . . disowning him." Hans even used scripture against his misguided boy. He reminded Luther of the fourth commandment, "Honor your father and mother!" Clearly Hans saw Luther's new direction as a vast waste of a costly education: his son was an investment that Hans expected some sort of return on. Hans felt betrayed and their relationship was badly strained.[16] In the 2003 movie *Luther*, directors Eric Till and Marc Canosa create a scene where Hans confronts his son after Luther's first mass as a priest. Luther tells his angry father that he had to go into the monastery because God, his heavenly Father, forced him to do so. Hans retorts, "A shaft of lightning burns your arse and you call that God? The Devil, more like!"

Only many years later after false rumors reached Hans that his friar son had died of the plague, would Hans's heart softened toward his boy again.[17] Despite the incredible pressure not to do so, Luther for good and for ill put

16. Brecht, *Martin Luther: 1483–1521*, 58.
17. Brecht, *Martin Luther: 1483–1521*, 58.

on the Augustinian cowl and with it the lifestyle of a friar. Convictions are like that. One day you are going along a well planned out road, and then something opens your eyes to a new reality. Luther seized on the moment, then came the doubts and anguish over his decision.[18]

Luther admitted that after he entered the monastery, he experienced what Germans call *Anfechtungen*, a deep inner spiritual anguish. We today might call it a debilitating depression rooted in a psychological obsession, but for Luther his despair focused largely upon the question of whether God loved him or not: it was a mania that unsettled Luther mentally, emotionally, and spiritually. Despite having followed his conscience into the monastery, he soon began to experience serious doubts over whether God had indeed been appeased by Luther's choice.[19]

In order to help Luther overcome his spiritual malaise, his superior and spiritual father, John Staupitz, put Luther on an academic path that Staupitz hoped might offer him some small comfort. Because of Luther's aptitude and passion for learning, Staupitz ordered his protégé to get a doctorate in theology and philosophy. Staupitz recognized that Luther especially enjoyed the study of scripture: the mentor hoped that God's word would ease his pupil's heart and mind.[20] As Luther engaged in the ASR and the study of biblical texts, after much doubt and years of mental anguish, he came to see God less as a vengeful deity and more as a gracious Lord. Luther's terror-filled conscience discovered a new focus, the pursuit of wisdom and truth. Luther equipped with new tools began to examine the way the religious world around him operated. His experience as a friar and his engagement with scripture raised serious questions in his mind about some church practices like indulgences.

Luther's studies led him to conclude that indulgences were not scriptural, but rather human-made policies of the church that furthered the fleecing the flock of their hard-earned coin, as he put it. Rather than offering the comfort of God's forgiveness, indulgences were a thinly veiled way of raising funds to build St. Peter's Basilica, which was being built in Rome at the time.

A new tension arose within his heart. As a loyal son of the church, who obeyed its traditions and teachings, he wished to support Catholicism, because it embodied the truth for Luther. However, his experience

---

18. WABr 2:238; LW 45:369, Loewenich, *Martin Luther*, 44.
19. Oberman, *Luther*, 226; Brecht, *Luther: 1483–1521*, 47, 68, 79–85.
20. Oberman, *Luther*, 314.

with the scriptures had raised some serious questions about whether the church at times was more interested in monetary gain than caring for its poorer members.[21]

Luther in 1510 was sent by Staupitz to Rome on official business for the Augustinian Order, in part because Staupitz believed a pilgrimage of this sort would help Luther confront his *Anfechtungen*. Rather it did the opposite and became a catalyst by which Luther's conscience determined to expose what he believed was the hypocrisy of indulgences. After dispatching his official duties, Luther went to visit the holy sites. Rome crawled with wayfarers from around the world anxiously scurrying about, visiting holy shrines, and doing penance to appease God. They often bought indulgences, so that their relatives might be freed from time in purgatory. Luther in many ways identified with the pilgrims and felt the same longing, because his grandfather had recently died. Luther even decided to buy him an indulgence and noted that he even he felt sorry that his parents were not yet dead, because as he put it, "I would have loved to deliver them from purgatory with my masses and other special works of prayer" by buying them indulgences as well.[22]

The indulgence Luther bought had two parts to it. Besides just purchasing a parchment that assured a spiritual release for his grandfather, Luther prayed while he crawled on his hands and knees up a stairway called the *Scala Sancta*—a set of twenty-eight white marble *Holy Steps*. These were purported to be the very steps Jesus climbed on the way up the praetorium to stand trial by the Governor Pontius Pilate (Matthew 27; Mark 15; Luke 23). Medieval legends suggest they were brought to Rome by the Emperor Constantine's mother, Helena, in the fourth century: they had been dismantled, taken to Rome, and reassembled next to the pope's church, the Archbasilica of St. John Lateran.

As Luther shuffled up the steps, praying a Lord's Prayer on every stair as charged, he noted that at first he had a strong feeling that his grandfather was being freed from agony. However, somewhere midway on his climb Luther tells us that his mind began to wander. In the words of Heiko Oberman, Luther wondered, "Would God allow himself to be pinned down this way?"[23] Would God really consider a few coins, a few Our Father's, and bruised knees to be an appropriate means of reconciliation for the guilt of

21. Oberman, *Luther*, 314.
22. Oberman, *Luther*, 147.
23. Oberman, *Luther*, 147.

sin? If forgiveness could be bought with coins, then didn't that mean that the rich had a distinct advantage over the poor? His conscience, which had been shaped by his studies, pricked his mind; something felt truly amiss.

It was no great sudden revelation of skepticism, notes Oberman, but a germination of an idea that had nagged at Luther for some time. A simple niggling thought, an apparent inconsequential idea, a question born out of conscience. Luther simply wondered, "Is this really true?"[24] His conscience answered, "No, it cannot be." And what began as a quest to save his grandfather from the purifying fires of purgatory, now ended in the conviction that there was something deeply wrong, not only with indulgences, but also with those who promoted them. Perhaps all formations of conscience start with the same simple niggling question, "Is this true?"

Notice that if Luther had been younger, he may not have questioned those in authority. Had he become a lawyer, perhaps even then he might not have had his doubts. But on account of his studies he had come to the conviction that it was *God's grace that saved*. Scripture had revealed it, his conscience clung to it as a core element of his belief, and so he decided to speak out and see if others felt the same way. He asked other scholars if he was right or wrong. If proven wrong, he would change his mind. If not, then the questions needed to be pursued.

In the ASR students often ask when looking at history and our present situation, "Why don't governments or religious institutions speak out more forcefully against social injustice, racism, poverty, a lack of healthcare for all, homelessness, sexism, human trafficking, climate change, or a host of other concerns?" Niggling questions arouse their consciences and motivate individuals to strive to make the world a better place. Deep down they are motivated by their religious and philosophical convictions that flow out what they learn in their majors. At some point, some students rise up and say, "No, I won't allow the world to continue on this path anymore. I will speak out and do something about it."

Social science students may raise concerns about how the mentally ill are treated or about government policies that disadvantage the poor. Science students may speak out about the ethics of certain medical practices, GMOs, cloning, global warning, chemical warfare, etc. Students in the arts may create art, music, and plays that create empathy for the outsider. English students do the same with poetry and literature. Passions flow from places of expertise, where people have tools that can be used to help society.

---

24. Oberman, *Luther*, 147.

Creating Conscience

Conscience pricks people to pick up the tools available to them to work against tyranny, even when it is not safe to do so.

For Luther, the day to take up his voice came on October 31, 1517. Pilgrims on the eve of All Saint's Day, November 1, traditionally flocked to holy sites around Europe to venerate relics, do penance, to attain indulgences. One of the most impressive collections of relics in Germany belonged to Luther's protector and lord, Duke Frederick of Saxony. Loewenich notes, "A visitor to [Frederick's] exhibit could receive a plenary indulgence of approximately two million years."[25] Luther had also come to see the attaining of indulgences by venerating relics as a similar problem to buying indulgences. Luther risked the wrath of his patron by speaking out against Frederick's indulgences from the pulpit.

Few, however, gave Luther, a young professor at an obscure college that had only recently been founded, much mind. His protestations early on did not have much impact. The status quo is always hard to overturn. So, on October 31, 1517 "out of a love of truth and in an effort to bring truth to light,"[26] Luther decided to take the conversation to another level. He wrote and published his Ninety-Five Theses, hoping for a public scholarly debate. Few notice.[27]

Luther in the very first thesis stated, "When our Lord and Master Jesus Christ said, 'Repent' (Matthew 4:17), he willed that the entire life of believers to be one of repentance."[28] If this was true, then wondered Luther, "What value did indulgences have?" In Luther's reading of the Bible, Jesus never demanded money when people repented, only heartfelt contrition and reformed lives. For Luther, the teachings of Jesus in the Gospels offered a simple and universal way to God. In one particularly impish thesis Luther asked, "Why does not the pope liberate everyone from purgatory for the sake of love (a most holy thing) and because of the supreme necessity of their souls? This would be morally the best of all reasons. Meanwhile he redeems innumerable souls for money, a most perishable thing, which to build St. Peter's church, a very minor purpose."[29]

A few enterprising publishers, as fate would have it, read Luther's theses and decided to translate them into the vernacular for all to read.

---

25. Loewenich, *Martin Luther*, 109.
26. Loewenich, *Martin Luther*, 109–10.
27. Oberman, *Luther*, 187–97.
28. Dillenberger, *Luther: Selections*, 490.
29. Thesis 82 in Dillenberger, *Luther: Selections*, 498.

They became a publishing phenomenon. People not only read but rallied to Luther's ideas and stopped buying indulgences. Once Luther's ideas affected the bottom line, and revenue from indulgences dropped off sharply in German lands, church officials finally took notice.[30]

The Ninety-Five Theses challenged indulgences and the motives of those who sold them, the church hierarchy. Luther perceived the abuses of indulgences as a type of oppression that was born out of a human error of judgment and greed. Luther's unassuming niggling questions had major ramifications, and some believe that Luther probably did not fully comprehended this at the time. Oberman suggests, "A historian can only call Luther's behavior intrepid—he did not evade condemnation by Rome and the empire.... At the beginning, it seemed a most remote possibility that this monk would ever leave his comfortable niche at the University of Wittenberg and set pope and emperor alike against him."[31] And yet, that's what happened. Luther thought that once Pope Leo X and others saw reason, they would rectify the situation. That did not happen.

Support for Luther's questions gained momentum among the German ruling class, who had always been skeptical of indulgences as just another way of extorting taxes out of the people. It soon became clear to pope and emperor that Luther's ideas, and the man, needed to be stopped. He had challenged their authority. Worse yet, financially things became difficult. Luther was summoned to the Diet of Worms in 1521. A Venetian diplomat at the Diet found the whole Luther affair ridiculous and a waste of time. The Diet had actually been called to deal with the Turks, who were threatening Europe. In other words, Luther had been summoned to a Diet that originally had nothing to do with him. The Diet rather had been called to focus upon the weighty matter of increasing taxes so that the Empire could go on crusade against Muslims, the Ottoman Turks, who threatened Europe. The Venetian legate concluded that Luther was nothing more than a "distraction from reality."[32] Oddly enough, that's the way consciences often work. They are distractions from reality—the status quo and the way things are normally done. Pricked consciences challenge oppressive societal norms, systemic injustices, and the powers that be do not take kindly to such pricking, especially if it impugns their integrity or thins their pocketbooks.

---

30. Oberman, *Luther*, 187–97.
31. Oberman, *Luther*, 187.
32. Oberman, *Luther*, 13.

Most people in power thought that silencing Luther quickly was the solution. And so, the little-known friar from Wittenberg was brought before Emperor Charles V to answer the charge of heresy. It was believed that Luther would wither under the regal might of the emperor, the political elite of Europe, and powerful representatives of Roman Catholic Church. Luther did find the whole affair disorienting, but nevertheless he clung to reason and scripture as a higher authority. Luther believed that God was revealed through the Bible and what he read in scripture went against indulgences and those who promoted them. Roman Catholic officials at Worms agreed that God was certainly known through scripture, but that the Bible was complicated and required the interpretive lens of Catholic tradition and teaching to be fully understood. If the pope, the primary spokesman for tradition and biblical truth, said indulgences were valid, then Luther needed to bow to such authority and fall in line or else suffer the consequences.[33]

What was Luther to do? He was after all, a faithful son of the church, an Augustinian friar, a priest, and a theologian of the Roman Catholic faith. If he, after careful examination of scripture and through clear reason came to a different conclusion than the tradition and the teachings of the church, then he was faced a crisis of conscience. Witnesses at Worms note that when Luther was asked to recant, he faltered and asked for a day to consider his answer. Many ignore this detail, but it seems to me to be consistent with the idea of conscience. At times, it is hard to know what is right, especially if two conflicting authorities reach an impasse. Luther had hoped for a debate, but there would be none of that.[34]

After a day Luther mustered his courage and responded in a clear and firm voice. Luther first begged his lords to forgive him, because, as an Augustinian friar accustomed to the monastic life, he admitted he was unfamiliar with such august proceedings. He feared he may already have offended some by his words and actions due to his lack of courtly manners. He hoped only to honor God and seek truth, he said. He acknowledged that he himself was far from being a saint, but nevertheless he had to remain true to his conscience.[35]

Luther again was asked to recant all his writings. Luther, however, noted that his books were of three different types. The first were spiritual works for the edification of the faithful and even his opponents and the

---

33. Oberman, *Luther,* 22–40.
34. Oberman, *Luther,* 22–40.
35. Oberman, *Luther,* 22–40.

papal bull that threatened him with excommunication admitted that they were without error and useful to those who read them. To recant these works would be to deny accepted Christian traditions and teachings. This, he said, was unthinkable because it would put his soul in peril. Second were his works against those who promoted ideas that were contrary to scripture and reason. To recant them would add "strength to tyranny and open not just a window, but the very doors, to un-Christian conduct."[36] Luther believed that if he recant these works, he would make himself a "tool of evil."[37] The last were directed against those who promoted "the tyranny of Rome and condemned godly teaching."[38] He regretted that at times he had been too harsh in his criticisms of individuals; after all, he admitted, he is human, and humans make mistakes. But the issue was not about how he said things, but about the truth. Nevertheless, Luther said that if he was shown according to scripture to be in error then he would gladly throw his books onto a pyre.[39]

What Luther did not talk about were the specific heretical charges brought against him. Rather he focused his response on the papacy, which promoted indulgences and obedience to traditions that he believed were not consistent with biblical texts. He had, in other words, kept to his core message and on this day at least he did not waver from his conscience.[40]

His questioners thought this answer evasive. They already had decided Luther was in error and a heretic, so all that remained was one simple question, "Will you recant?" They wanted a straightforward answer. Luther was not to give any more speeches. Would he submit to the authority of the church or not? And so, Luther gave them his answer in Latin so all could understand:

> Since then, your serene majesty and your lordships seek a simple answer, I will give it in this manner, neither horned or untoothed: unless I am convinced by the testimony of the scriptures or by clear reason (for I do not trust either in the pope or in councils alone, since it is well known that they have often erred and contradicted themselves), I am bound by the scriptures and my

---

36. Loewenich, *Martin Luther*, 194.
37. Brecht, *Martin Luther 1483–1521*, 458.
38. Loewenich, *Martin Luther*, 194.
39. Brecht, *Martin Luther 1483–1521*, 459.
40. Brecht, *Martin Luther 1483–1521*, 459.

conscience which is captive to the Word of God. I cannot and I will not recant, to go against conscience is neither right nor safe.

Then he added in German almost as if to himself, "God help me! Amen." Some printed versions of this text later added the words, "Here I stand, I can do no other."[41] It is worthy of note that Luther clearly linked his conscience with reasoned argument. "Pure reason" requires critical thinking, which in turn reveals truth. If a tradition, teaching, or policy is experienced as tyrannical, it must be exposed, or so Luther argued. Critical and plain reasoning reveals truth and cannot abide falsehood.

The ASR also appeals to reasoned critical argument, which demands close examination of one's own assumptions and the authorities that one appeals to. In our present age of "fake news" getting at truth has become an even more critical issue than when I first started teaching thirty years ago. Some politicians believe that truth is what they say it is. Their followers have established entire news channels, radio programs, internet chat rooms, newspapers, and electronic websites that repeat their claims without critical analysis. They demand unthinking obedience. Like a few leaders in Luther's day, who argued along a similar line of reasoning, leaders today at times do not want the truth exposed, because it does not shed a good light on them. It does not benefit them financially or otherwise. But conscience pursues pure reason and will not abide double-speak, which Orwell warned us about in *1984*.

Likewise, we all take for granted, like the air around us, what authorities we rest our convictions and consciences upon. We develop our opinions and our consciences out of experience and then look for authorities that support our worldview. The ASR helps us to think more clearly about what our assumptions are and whether or not we are blindly following ideas that promote injustice or not. It helps us to think critically about why we and others believe what we believe. In so doing, those who speak of religion can think more clearly about and even clarify what their consciences are telling them. In turn, at times, we may even discover our passions in life as we explore our deepest convictions. Like Luther, we may have our doubts when we embark upon a path, but if even if we falter, we need to follow our consciences. In so doing, we at least have the hope of finding meaningful direction in life.

Nothing is sadder than a deeply held conviction that has no basis in reason or rests upon an authority that seeks anything less that the good of

---

41. Loewenich, *Martin Luther*, 195, translation slightly altered.

all. History is littered with people who think they are doing the will of God or their ideology, which they have confused with their own will, as they perpetrate injustice. What terrible abuses and unspeakable acts of cruelty have been committed in the name of religion or philosophical ideals? How often have people used mental gymnastics of Olympian proportions to suggest that fear and hatred are really the love of God and in so doing have justified the condemnation of others. How often have minorities, immigrants, and the poor suffered under such cruelty. Such Machiavellian arguments claim that the end justifies the means, and thus violence, vigilantism, and state-sanctioned terrorism are claimed to be the way to peace. Simple truth exposes such ironic irenic logic. However, when such views become a part of the daily normal, many do not see that they support the oppression of those of different races, sexual orientations, genders, or faith traditions. Rather, they see it as a freedom to enslave, a right to take matters into their own hands, and requirement to persecute those they deem as threats to their way of life.

Sometimes the opposite is the problem. Some who undertake the ASR don't want to be bothered by conscience and so they may say, "But when it comes to religion, it doesn't matter what you believe." The ASR addresses this point head on because people can mean a variety of things by it. At best, they imply that it is essential when speaking of religion to follow one's conscience: this fits the goals of the ASR. However, few have this in mind when they make this declaration. Usually when I press students on the point, they are really trying to dismiss the enterprise of the ASR, because they want to embrace their ignorance. It becomes a way of saying, "The ASR doesn't matter because we can believe what we want." However, when pushed, all students quickly backtrack from this position, realizing that when they think about it reasonably, they don't really believe the declaration. If what they mean by this is some sort of religious or philosophical free for all, anything goes, then such reasoning is easily exposed as wanting. Is it okay to be a so-called "Christian Nazi," as many white supremacists claim to be, who seeks to rid the world of Jews or Africans by violent means? Of course not. There are hateful and murderous convictions in the world, which must not be allowed a credibility that is equal to compassionate religious traditions and teachings. The two are opposite realities. One deals with the best of religion and the other seeks to exploit religion to justify hatred and even at times genocide.

Creating Conscience

Therefore, it is a central tenet of the ASR to distinguish between compassionate and non-compassionate traditions. Religions or ideologies that are based on fear are defined by what and who they hate. At the heart of the ASR is compassionate, convicted, and civil religious and philosophical traditions, teachings, and experiences. The ASR exposes violent religious views for what they are. We may study such malicious convictions—for example, racist views that exist systemically in, say, churches, other social institutions, and governments—but if we allow such vicious views a place of honor alongside loving religious worldviews, as if there is no difference between them, then the ASR has lost its way.

When Martin Luther's conscience spoke, he realized that there was nothing for it, he could not retreat into silence or submission with good reasons for doing so. When the church he loved asked him to contradict his conscience, he could not do so, even if it meant death. Luther in the end concluded that saving his own skin was not a compelling enough reason to go against his conscience. To go against a loving conscience is to give up on being yourself.

Our consciences may not ever need to ask of us to put our lives on the line, but it is quite probable that there will come times in our lives when we must stand up for others and in so doing, we will suffer the emotional attacks of others. It may even cost us our jobs, prestige, honor, a bonus, or some other reward, but when the time comes, standing on conscience for the good of others will always be the right thing to do. Be ready. When a conscience pricks and you speak out, you will likely be asked to step back in line, hold our tongue, get with the program, and stop rocking the boat. Such phrases are tactics, tools of leaders who do not want to be challenged to do the right thing. They want to keep on doing their thing. They expect us to ignore indiscretions; they say that they didn't mean it, even though it has happened before, often many times. Whenever anyone suffers, we all suffer—we will never be free until all are free, suggested Dr. Martin Luther King. The truth is no less true today than it was yesterday. I do not know when you will be asked to compromise your conscience, but I do know the time will come. The ASR helps you to be ready for that day so we can take up whatever tools we have to change the tyranny the rises up in our lives.

I have told this to students for decades, namely that someday they will need to make a choice based on conscience. I have said that they will be asked to go along with the system and not expose abuse. It can happen in a myriad of ways, sometimes it is subtle and at other times overt, but just

Speaking of Religion . . .

remember I told you so. Remember that the moment of truth is out there hurtling at you, and you will need to decide what your ultimate concern is that motivates you to act. I have had students tell me years after I've had them in class, "It happened . . ." and then they tell the story. In all these instances, they were life-defining moments, situations where they had to choose compassion over ignorance or neglect, conviction over conforming to a compromise, civility over picking a side against the downtrodden. I would give examples, but in each instance my former students would be able to see themselves in the comments. Let me leave it at this. The time will come, and you will know when it is, that your turn to stand on conscience is needed. Being forewarned is to prepare for the moment of truth. Being forewarned allows us to imagine a response now, so that when it happens, we will simply say, "Here I stand, I can do no other."

The emperor condemned Luther as an outlaw, and his punishment could have been the stake, but Luther had been given safe passage to Worms and so he returned to Germany where he continued to seek reforms throughout the rest of his life. But an important caveat must be made at this point. I must acknowledge that many when writing about Luther often leave him as a hero of conscience, because we all need a positive model to value. I understand this temptation, but there is much more to this story, that still needs to be told. In fact, it would not be complete without the whole truth.

Luther later would himself become a part of the established system. German rulers in places broke with Rome and they asked Luther to help them imagine how to restructure their lands. Over time, Luther came to use his conscience on at least two other major occasions to oppress others. They involved Luther's lack of support for the peasants seeking justice against harsh lords and the Jews hoping Luther would help their own stand on conscience against ruthless demands for them to convert to Christianity. It is a sad reality that Luther actively promoted views that led to the deaths of countless peasants and Jews alike. Today, I and we must condemn in the strongest possible terms Luther's indifference to the consciences of the peasants and Jews, who both at some point or other appealed to Luther for help in their plight. One might imagine that Luther would have been more sympathetic given what he had been through, but in the end, he was not.

The full story is told in many other books but let me briefly point out that Luther himself refused to lift a finger to help the peasants when they revolted.[42] Also, he promoted anti-Judaic and anti-Semitic attitudes and

---

42. Baylor, *German Reformation and the Peasants' War*; Oberman, *Luther*, 277–83.

laws that are a remarkable blight on his memory. In short, with regard to the Jews, Luther believed that they should abandon their consciences and convert to Christianity. If you read his work *On the Jews and Their Lies*, you will see that Luther encourages Protestants to take seven specific actions against the Jews if they do not convert: 1. to burn their synagogues and schools, 2. to not allow them to own houses or property in Christian communities, 3. to take their Jewish religious texts from them, 4. to keep rabbis from teaching and preaching, 5. to refuse them protection as they traveled on highways, 6. to prohibit the practice of usuary and to take their gold and silver and only return them if they converted to Christianity, and 7. to force strong young Jews into hard labor to earn their bread.[43]

Just why Luther took these stands also demands more time than we have here. Let it suffice to say, that once Luther's reformation won the support of nobles and lords, Luther became convinced of the rightness of his cause, and did not tolerate those who posed a threat to him and his ideas. Not even their appeal to their consciences moved him. He became rigid in his rightness, he forgot compassion towards all, and turned his version of the truth into an oppressive weapon against his enemies. Luther's legacy is forever tainted by his failings in this regard.

It should come as no surprise that Hitler praised Luther's anti-Semitic writings and even reprinted and distributed them widely during the days of Nazi Germany. It is no accident that *Kristallnacht*, "the night of broken glass," on November 9-10, 1938, occurred on Luther's birthday, because Nazi's hailed his ideas as foundational of their own. Indeed, Luther's bequest of hatred is not over, since many white supremacist groups still point to Luther's ideas as a basis of their own views. Again, Luther in this sense must be renounced in the strongest possible terms over and over again.[44]

Thus, Luther's development of conscience here is lifted up as a double-edged example. In part, it can reveal how conscience is formed and properly be appealed to, but Luther also reveals that conscience can go astray, much more easily than we think. Luther's story is a cautionary tale. Perhaps the final point is that a compassionate conscience demands nothing less than a lifetime of struggle, critical thinking, heartfelt conviction, civility, and a rigorous pursuit of the truth, alongside regular self-examination so that we ourselves do not lose our way.

---

43. Martin Luther, "*On the Jews and Their Lies*" in LW 47:268-71.

44. For more on this see Oberman, *The Roots of Anti-Semitism* and Kaufmann, *Luther's Jews*.

Conclusion
Living the Questions

"A faithful study of the liberal arts
humanizes character and permits it not to be cruel."
Ovid (d. 18 CE)

—*Publius Ovidius Naso*, Ex Ponto, II, ix, 47

"Education is the point at which we decide whether we
love the world enough to assume responsibility for it."

—Hannah Arendt (d. 1975), *The Crisis of Education*

Two thousand years ago, the Roman poet Ovid (d. 18 CE) starkly suggested that the goal of the liberal arts, of which the ASR is a part, is to humanize character so that it will not be cruel. Put more positively, the ASR pursues compassionate wisdom and not just the simple accumulation of information to pass a test. This is no easy endeavor. Perhaps one of the most challenging aspects of the ASR is that it requires, at the very least, humility. Helmut Thielicke warns, "Truth seduces us very easily into a kind of joy of possession: I have comprehended this and that, learned it, understood it. Knowledge is power ... but love is the opposite of the will to possess. It is self-giving. It boasteth not itself, but humbleth itself."[1] G. K. Chesterton once famously quipped, "The reason angels can fly is because

---

1. Thielicke, *A Little Exercise*, 38.

they take themselves lightly."[2] For Thielicke and Chesterton, humility is the virtue of taking ourselves lightly and in so doing we are enabled, especially through education, to rise up beyond earthbound self-interest to the stars of empathy. Humility underpins our hope for a brighter future that can be built out of compassionate, convicted civility. The ills of any society are always rooted in the bravado of pride: leaders lording and placing themselves above the law and others; the rich gaining, draining economic and emotional resources way from the have-nots.

Lewis B. Smedes has pointed out that it is only through humble convictions, passionate resolve, and imagination that any real hope enters our world. Before it is possible, a gentler world must first be envisaged by means of the imagination: we must dream of a future without racial, sexual, or religious discrimination. A world where harmony flourishes amid religious diversity and true equality exists for all. Once imagined, a compassionate justice can embolden our passions to seek after what has always eluded us. It all begins with the power of one; the heart of an individual person, who does what she can, where she is in the world, with the tools that are at her disposal. The power of the one awakens other sleepy hearts to caring actions born out of conscience. From one person's vision, a neighborhood comes together, and ultimately communities transform lands.[3] As my favorite theologian, Gandalf the wizard, has so astutely observed, "[Some believe] it is only great power that can hold evil in check, but that is not what I have found. It is the small everyday deeds of ordinary folk that keep the darkness at bay. Small acts of kindness and love."[4] The ASR empowers individuals to think creatively, to see imaginatively, and to act decisively in pursuit of compassionate, convicted, and civil communities.

Martha Nussbaum, discussing the importance of the humanities in education, has said that "the bureaucratization of social life and the relentless machinelike character of modern states has deadened people's moral imaginations, leading them to acquiesce in atrocities with no twinge of conscience."[5] Our failure in the past has often been a failure of imagination: without it, sympathy is not possible, empathy is dismissed as idealism, and understanding is set aside as impractical. Those who think otherwise are

---

2. Chesterton, *Collected Works*, vol. 1, 126.

3. Smedes, *Standing on the Promises*, 11–25.

4. This Gandalf quote is from the movie, *The Hobbit: An Unexpected Journey* (2012), directed by Peter Jackson.

5. Nussbaum, *Not For Profit*, 54.

often called dreamers or out of touch with the "real" world. But what could be more real than seeing the world for what it really is and striving for what it should be? The ASR opens the eyes of our moral vision, ennobling us with ideals that are born out of our deepest religious and philosophical hopes.

The ASR is a never-ending journey, a long pilgrim path toward answers that may never be fully realized in this life. The joy of transforming our troubled world into a beloved community may only be grasped weakly, but it is possible because people like Dr. Martin Luther King Jr. have dreamed it and shown it to us. We often may become impatient or disheartened by the enormity of the tasks that stretches out before us. We may push for immediate answers to troubling questions, and regularly become discouraged at the slow pace of change in the world. Despite all our good efforts to find solutions to our problems, real answers often elude us. Rainer Maria Rilke's advice to a young poet is most fitting at this point:

> Be patient toward all that is unsolved in your heart and try to love the questions themselves, like locked rooms and like books that are now written in a very foreign tongue. Do not now seek the answers, which cannot be given you because you would not be able to live them. And the point is, to live everything. Live the questions now. Perhaps you will then gradually, without noticing it, live along some distant day into the answer.[6]

The quest for truth seeks after the mysterious holy grail of wisdom. The smallest spark of wisdom can enflame a conscience allowing it to burn bright amid the night of everyday suffering. We dare not embark on such an adventure alone, lest life's perils on the path overcome us. It is better by far to venture forth in a community of diverse explorers, compassionate companions, who will both challenge and encourage us along the way. Then, and only then, will our hopes for the beloved community be born amid all the wonderful difference of diversity that this world has to offer. As we come together to speak of religion in the hallway of the ASR, we will find a way to compassionate, convicted, and civil lives.

---

6. Rilke, *Letters to a Young Poet*, 27.

"Truth is a lion.
You don't have to defend it.
Let it loose.
It will defend itself."

—Falsely attributed to St. Augustine, (d. 430)
but true, nonetheless.

Bibliography

A Common Word. Online: https://www.acommonword.com/.
Alexander, Elizabeth. Online: http://www.elizabethalexander.net/front-page-1 and https://onbeing.org/programs/desire-know-elizabeth-alexander-2/.
Armstrong, Karen. *The Bible: The Biography.* New York: Atlantic Monthly, 2007.
Augustine. *City of God.* London: Penguin Classics, 2004.
———. *Confessions.* Oxford: Oxford University Press, 2009.
Baylor, Michael C. *The German Reformation and the Peasants' War: A Brief History with Documents.* Boston: Bedford, 2012.
Bonhoeffer, Dietrich. *The Cost of Discipleship.* New York: Touchstone, 1995.
Bragova, Arina. "Cicero on the Gods and Roman Religious Practices." *Studia Antiqua et Archeologica* 23.2 (2017) 303–13.
Brecht, Martin. *Martin Luther: His Road to Reformation 1483–1521.* Philadelphia: Fortress, 1985.
Chesterton, G. K. Illustrated. *London News* September 11, 1909. In *The Collected Works of G. K. Chesterton.* San Francisco: Ignatius, 1992.
———. *Orthodoxy.* Bellingham, WA: Lexham, 2017.
———. *The Collected Works of G. K. Chesterton, Vol. 1: Heretics, Orthodoxy, the Blatchford Controversy.* San Francisco: Ignatius, 1986.
Cunningham, Lawrence, and John Kelsay. *The Sacred Quest: An Invitation to the Study of Religion.* New York: Pearson, 2013.
Darwin, Charles. *On the Origins of the Species by Means of Natural Selection, or the Preservation of Favoured Races in the Struggle for Life.* 2nd ed. London: John Murray, 1860.
Doheny, Kathleen. "Depression on the Rise in Colleges?" *WebMD.* Online: https://www.webmd.com/mental-health/news/20100812/depression-on-the-rise-in-colleges#1.
Eck, Diana, *Encountering God: A Spiritual Journey from Bozeman to Banaras.* New York: Beacon, 2003.
———. Interview in "Pluralism Project Celebrates Silver Anniversary." *The Harvard Gazette,* September 16, 2016. Online: https://news.harvard.edu/gazette/story/newsplus/pluralism-project-celebrates-silver-anniversary/.
———. *A New Religious America.* San Francisco: HarperSanFrancisco, 2001.
Freud, Sigmund. *The Future of an Illusion.* New York: Norton, 1990.
Harding, Vincent. *Hope and History: Why We Share the Story of a Movement.* Maryknoll, NY: Orbis, 2009.
———. *Martin Luther King: The Inconvenient Hero.* Maryknoll, NY: Orbis, 2008.

Bibliography

———. *There is a River: The Black Struggle for Freedom in the Americas*. San Diego: Harcourt Brace & Co., 1981.

Harrison, Peter. *Narratives of Secularization*. London: Routledge, 2017.

———. *The Territories of Science and Religion*. Chicago: University of Chicago Press, 2017.

———. "Why Religion Is Not Going Away and Science Will Not Destroy It." *Aeon*. Online: https://getpocket.com/explore/item/why-religion-is-not-going-away-and-science-will-not-destroy-it?utm_source=pocket-newtab.

Harrison, Peter, and Jon Roberts, eds, *Science without God: Rethinking the History of Scientific Naturalism*. Oxford: Oxford University Press, 2019.

Hügel, Friedrich von. *The Mystical Elements of Religion: As Studied in Saint Catherine of Genoa and Her Friends*. 2 vols. London: Dent & Sons, 1908, revised 1923.

James, William. *The Varieties of Religious Experience*. New York: Modern Library, 1929.

Kaufmann, Thomas. *Luther's Jews: A Journey into Anti-Semitism*. Oxford: Oxford University Press, 2017.

Keeble, N. H. "C. S. Lewis, Richard Baxter, and 'Mere Christianity.'" *Christianity and Literature* XXX.3 (1981) 27–44.

King in the Wilderness. Documentary. Directed by Peter Kunhardt. HBO, 2018.

King Jr, Martin Luther. *Strength to Love*. Minneapolis: Fortress, 2010.

Lactantius. *Firmiani Lactantii Epitome Institutionum Divinarum: Lactantius' Epitome of the Divine Institutes*. Eugene, OR: Wipf and Stock, 2010.

Leonard, Ellen M., "Friedrich von Hügel's Spirituality of Empowerment." *Horizons* 21.2 (1994) 270–87.

Levin, Yuval. "The Moral Challenge of Modern Science." *The New Atlantis: A Journal of Technology & Society* (Fall 2006) 32–46. Online: https://www.thenewatlantis.com/publications/the-moral-challenge-of-modern-science.

Lewis, Charlton T. *An Elementary Latin Dictionary*. Oxford: Oxford University Press, 1963.

Lewis, C. S., *Mere Christianity*. San Francisco: Harper Collins, 2001.

———. *Spirits in Bondage: A Cycle of Lyrics*. New York: Cosimo Classics, 2005.

———. *Surprised by Joy: The Shape of My Early Life*. New York: Harcourt Brace Jovanovich, 1966.

Lewis, W. H. ed. *The Letters of C. S. Lewis*. New York: Harcourt Brace Jovanovich, 1966.

Lipka, Michael. "A Closer Look at America's Rapidly Growing Religious 'Nones.'" Pew Research Center May 13, 2015. Online: https://www.pewresearch.org/fact-tank/2015/05/13/a-closer-look-at-americas-rapidly-growing-religious-nones/.

Loewenich, Walther von. *Martin Luther: The Man and His Work*. Minneapolis: Augsburg, 1982.

Lohse, Bernard. *Martin Luther: An Introduction to His Life and Works*. Philadelphia: Fortress, 1986.

Luo, Michael. "American Christianity's White Supremacy Problem." *The New Yorker Magazine*, September 2, 2020. Online: https://www.newyorker.com/books/under-review/american-christianitys-white-supremacy-problem.

Luther, Martin. *Luther's Works* (LW). 55 vols. Minneapolis: Fortress and Concordia, 1957.

———. *Martin Luther: Selections from His Writings*. Edited by John Dillenberger. New York: Anchor, 1958.

———. *Weimar Ausgabe* (WA). Online: http://www.lutherdansk.dk/WA/D.%20Martin%20Luthers%20Werke,%20Weimarer%20Ausgabe%20-%20WA.htm.

Bibliography

———. *Weimar Briefe* (WABr). Online: http://www.lutherdansk.dk/WA/D.%20Martin%20Luthers%20Werke,%20Weimarer%20Ausgabe%20-%20WA.htm.

Marty, Martin. *By Way of Response*. Nashville: Abingdon, 1981.

Marty, Martin, with Jonathan Moore. *Education, Religion and the Common Good: Advancing a Distinctly American Conversation about Religion's Role in Our Shared Life*. San Francisco: Jossey-Bass, 2000.

Marx, Karl. "A Contribution to the Critique of Hegel's Philosophy of Right." Online: https://www.marxists.org/archive/marx/works/download/Marx_Critique_of_Hegels_Philosophy_of_Right.pdf.

McGrath, Alister. *C. S. Lewis: A Life*. Carol Stream, IL: Tyndale House, 2013.

Miles, Margaret R. *Augustine and the Fundamentalist's Daughter*. Eugene, OR: Cascade, 2011.

MLK/FBI. Documentary. Directed by Sam Pollard. Depth of Vision/Tradecraft Films, 2020. Online: https://www.mlkfbi.co.uk/.

Mouw, Richard. *Uncommon Decency: Christian Civility in an Uncivil World*. Downers Grove, IL: InterVarsity, 2010.

Newberg, Andrew, Eugene d'Aquili, and Vince Rouse. *Why God Won't Go Away*. New York: Ballantine, 2002.

Newberg, Andrew and Mark Robert Waldman. *Why We Believe What We Believe: Uncovering Our Biological Need for Meaning, Spirituality, and Truth*. New York: Free, 2006.

Norton Anthology of Poetry. New York: Norton, 2006.

Nussbaum, Martha. *Not for Profit: Why Democracy Needs the Humanities*. Princeton: Princeton University Press, 2010.

Oberman, Heiko. *Luther: Man between God and the Devil*. New Haven, CT: Yale University Press, 1982.

———. *The Roots of Anti-Semitism in the Age of Renaissance and Reformation*. Minneapolis: Fortress, 1984.

Online Etymological Dictionary. Online: https://www.etymonline.com/.

Patel, Eboo. *Acts of Faith: The Story of an American Muslim, the Struggle for the Soul of a Generation*. New York: Beacon, 2007.

Pratt, Douglass. "Exclusivism and Exclusivity: A Contemporary Theological Challenge." *Pacifica* 20.3 (2007) 291–306.

Rilke, Rainer Maria. *Letters to a Young Poet*. New York: Norton, 1993.

Sagan, Carl. *The Demon-Haunted World*. New York: Ballantine, 1997.

Schmidt, Benjamin. "The Humanities Are in Crisis." *Atlantic*, August 28, 2018. Online: https://www.theatlantic.com/ideas/archive/2018/08/the-humanities-face-a-crisisof-confidence/567565/.

Shelton, Jason E. *Blacks and Whites in Christian America: How Racial Discrimination Shapes Religious Convictions*. New York: New York University Press, 2012.

Smedes, Lewis B. *Standing on the Promises: Keeping Hope Alive for a Tomorrow We Cannot Control*. Nashville: Thomas Nelson, 1998.

Smith, Christian. *Divided by Faith: Evangelical Religion and the Problem of Race in America*. Oxford: Oxford University Press, 2001.

Smith, Kenneth L., and Ira G. Zepp Jr. *Search for the Beloved Community: The Thinking of Martin Luther King Jr*. King of Prussia, PA: Judson, 1998.

Swidler, Leonard, and Paul Moizes. *The Study of Religion in an Age of Global Dialogue*. Philadelphia: Temple University Press, 2000.

Bibliography

Taylor, Barbara Brown. *Holy Envy: God in the Faith of Others*. New York: HarperOne, 2019.
Thielicke, Helmut. *A Little Exercise for Young Theologians*. Grand Rapids: Eerdmans,1962.
Tillich, Paul. *Dynamics of Faith*. New York: HarperOne, 2009.
———. *Systematic Theology*. 3 vols. Chicago: University of Chicago Press, 1973–76.
Tippett, Krista. "On Being: Civil Conversations." Online: http://www.civilconversationsproject.org/.
Tolkien, J. R. R. *The Fellowship of the Ring*. New York: Ballantine, 1986.
Ungureanu, James C. "A Yankee at Oxford: John William Draper at the British Association for the Advancement of Science at. Oxford, 30 June 1860." *Notes and Records: The Royal Society Journal of History of Science*. Online: https://doi.org/10.1098/rsnr.2015.0053.
Wallace, Anthony F. C. *Religion: An Anthropological View*. New York: Random House, 1966.
War Relocation Authority 1946. The Evacuated People: A Quantitative Study. Online: http://npshistory.com/publications/incarceration/evacuated-people.pdf.
Ware, Kallistos. *The Orthodox Way*. Yonkers, NY: St. Vladimir's Seminary Press, 2019.
World Health Organization. Online: https://www.who.int/health-topics/human-rights#tab=tab_1.

Index

1860 Oxford Evolution Debate, 8
95 Theses, *See* Ninety-Five Theses of Martin Luther.

A Common Word (Interfaith Document Against Terrorism), 74–75
Agnosticism, 4, 16, 29, 39, 69, 93
Alexander, Elizabeth, 82
Anfechtungen (Martin Luther's Spiritual Depression), 102–3
Anselm of Canterbury, 6
Anti-Semitism, 112–13, 120–21
Arendt, Hannah, 114
Armstrong, Karen, 9
Ataturk, Mustafa Kemal, 12
Atheism, 4, 9–10, 16, 18, 20–21, 27, 29, 39, 69, 82, 93, 96–98
Augustine of Hippo, 2, 7, 40, 52, 117

Baylor, Michael, 112
Baxter, Richard, 68
Beloved Community, 89–91, 116
Biblical Literalism. *See* Literal Interpretation of Scripture.
Blakemore, Colin, 11
Bonhoeffer, Dietrich, 26, 28
Bragova, Arina, 7
Brecht, Martin, 101–2, 108
Buber, Martin, 27
Buddhism, 23, 37, 40–41, 61, 69
Bush, George, 12

Canosa, Marc, 101
Catholicism, 8, 14–16, 19, 22, 26–27, 31–32, 36–37, 68–69, 73, 98, 102, 107

Charles V (Emperor), 107, 112
Chesterton, G. K., 18, 44, 89, 114–15
Christianity, 3–7, 10, 14, 17–29, 31–32, 36–37, 40–75, 82–89, 97–98, 105, 108, 110, 112–13
Cicero, 6–7
Common Word. See A Common Word.
Comte, Auguste, 11
Communism, Russian, 10, 12, 25
Conscience, 92–116
Constantine I, the Great, 103
Convicted Civility, 3–5, 30–32, 38, 42–43, 66–67, 72, 77, 87, 89–90, 112–13, 115
Cunningham, Lawrence, 32

d'Aquili, Eugene, 17
Darwin, Charles, 8–12
Dawkins, Richard, 11
Day, Dorothy, 27
de Montaigne, Michel, 67
Depression, 40, 59, 102
Dialogue Rules, 73–74
Diet of Worms, 92, 98, 106–8
Dillenberger, John, 105
Doctrine (General Term), 13, 21, 35, 52, 69
Doctrine/Teaching (Friedrich von Hügel's Second Aspect of Religion), 20–23
Doheny, Kathleen, 40

Eck, Diana, 77–82, 85–86, 94
Evangelical Christians, 3, 32, 36, 82, 87
Exclusivism, 20, 27, 80–87

Index

Experience/Mysticism (Fredrich von Hügel Third Aspect of Religion), 14–16, 21–32

Fake News, 109
Fans and Fanatics, 18, 28
Frederick the Wise, 105
Freud, Sigmund, 9–11

Gandalf (Lord of the Rings), 115
Gandhi, Mahatma, 26
Gbowee, Leymah, 27
Goodall, Jane, 26
Guillaume de Lorris, 30

Helena (Mother of Constantine I), 103
Herbert, George, 67
Humanities in Crisis, 11, 34–35, 115
Hammerling, Roy (Case Study), 45–51
Harding, Vincent, 89
Harris, Samuel, 11
Harrison, Peter 11–12
Hawking, Stephen, 11
Hinduism, 17–18, 23, 26, 40, 69, 80, 82
Hoover, J. Edgar, 25
Hügel, Friedrich von, 8, 12–25
Hughes, Howard, 95
Humility, 37, 39, 57, 76, 78, 114–15
Huxley, Thomas Henry, 9

Incarceration of Japanese Citizens, 88
Inclusivism, 80–82, 85
Indulgences, 102–8
Iqbal, Allama Muhammad, 82
Islam, 12, 16–19, 21, 23, 26, 31, 34, 36–37, 40–45, 58, 61–63, 69–72, 74–75, 78, 80, 82–85, 88, 106

James, William, 7–8
Jean de Meun, 30
Jesus, 15, 22, 25–26, 32, 42, 48–49, 52, 55–56, 59, 68, 82, 97, 103, 105
Jews and Judaism, 9–10, 16–19, 21, 23, 25–27, 31, 34, 36–37, 40–42, 48, 58, 69, 72, 75, 82, 87, 110, 112–13
Joan of Arc, 26

Karman, Tawakkai, 27
Kaufman, Thomas, 113

Kazantzakis, Nikos, 27
Keeble, N. H., 68
Keller, Helen, 44
Kelsay, John, 32
King, Dr. Martin Luther, 25–26, 50, 89–92, 116
Kingsley, Charles, 8
Khrushchev, Nikita, 10

Lactantius, 7
Leonard, Ellen, 13–14
Levin, Yuval, 13–14
Lewis, C. S., 5, 33, 67–70, 82, 96–97
Lewis, W. H., 82
LGBTQ+, 27, 43, 63–66, 86
Lipka, Michael, 29
Literal Interpretation of Scripture, 4, 9, 17, 48–49
Lohse, Bernard, 100
Loewenich, Walther von, 98–100, 102, 105, 108–9
Lord's Prayer, 103
Luo, Mark, 75
Luther, Hans (Martin Luther's father), 98–99, 101
Luther, Martin, 52, 92, 98–113
Luther, Margarethe (Martin Luther's Mother, a.k.a. Hannah), 98
Lutheranism, 17, 20, 25–28, 31–32, 39, 45–46, 50–58, 61, 64, 89–93, 98–113, 116

Marty, Martin, 4–5, 21, 33, 37, 89
Marx, Karl, 10–11
McGrath, Alister, 96
McCarthyism, 88
Mechú, Rigoberta, 27
Michelangelo di Lodovico Buonarroti Simoni, 15
Miles, Margaret, 46
Moizes, Paul, 73
Moral Majority, 3
Mouw, Richard, 5, 87–89
Muhammad ibn Abdullah, 42–43, 61
Muslims. *See* Islam.
Mysticism (Fredrich von Hügel Third Aspect of Religion). *See* Experience.

Index

Nazi Ideology, 11, 23, 26, 28, 68, 75, 87–88, 110, 113
Newberg, Andrew, 17–19, 27–28, 43
Ninety-Five Theses of Martin Luther, 105–6
Nones, *See* Pew Research Center.
Nkom, Alice, 27
Nussbaum, Martha Craven, 35–36, 115

Oberman, Heiko, 99, 102–7, 112–13
Orthodoxy, Eastern, 27, 32, 37, 68–69
Orthodoxy, Russian, 12, 34
Orwell, George, 109
Ovid, (Publius Ovidus Naso), 114

Pakistan (Wasir Kahn Mosque, Lahore), 83
Papenfuss, Hannah (Case Study), 58–61
Papenfuss, Luke (Case Study), 63–65
Patel, Eboo, 78–79
Pew Research Center (Nones), 28–29
Plato, ix
Pluralism, 79–82
Pontius Pilate, 103
Pratt, Douglass, 81
Prayer, 14, 40, 45–46, 69–71, 82–86, 96, 99, 103
Protestantism, 10, 28, 32, 36–37, 69, 105, 113

Rabin, Yitzhak, 26
Race/Racism, 4, 13, 25, 41–43, 46, 50, 57, 75, 86–87, 89–93, 104, 110
Rifai, Emma (Case Study), 54–58
Rilke, Rainer Maria, 116
Roberts, Jon, 12
Rohde, Sarah (Case Study), 51–54
Romance of the Rose, 30
Rouse, Vince, 121

Sagan, Carl, 12
Scala Sancta (Holy Steps), 103
Secular/Secularization, 9, 11–12, 18, 21, 54–58,
Schmidt, Benjamin, 34
Shakespeare, William, 31
Shelton, Jason E., 89

Sikhs, 18, 40, 80
Smedes, Lewis B., 115
Smith, Christian, 2–3
Smith, Kenneth, 121
Soelle (Sölle), Dorothee, 52
Socrates, 26, 33
Swidler, Leonard, 73–74
Staupitz, John, 102–3

Taylor, Barbara Brown, 71
Teaching (Friedrich von Hügel's Second Aspect of Religion), *See* Doctrine.
Thielicke, Helmut, 4, 6, 77, 114–15
Till, Eric, 101
Tillich, Paul, 17, 93, 96, 100
Tippett, Krista, 78, 87
Tolerance, 2, 78, 80, 113
Tolkien, J.R.R., 1–2
Toumeh, Nadia (Case Study), 61–63
Tradition (Friedrich von Hügel First Aspect of Religion), 14–20
Tradition, 4, 14–37, 41–43, 46, 49–50, 56, 61, 64, 68–69, 71–72, 74–75, 80–82, 85, 98, 105, 107–11
Truth, 4, 7, 9, 11–16, 20, 23, 27–28, 31, 33, 37, 42, 45–46, 48, 50, 54, 70, 77, 80–81, 84, 90–91, 97, 102, 104–5, 107–17
Truth, Sojourner, 27

Ungureanu, James C., 9

Waldman, Mark Robert, 17–19, 27, 43
Wallace, Anthony F. C., 11
War of Roses, 30
War Relocation Authority 1946, 88
Ware, Kallistos (born Timothy Richard), 32
White Supremacy, 25, 75, 110, 113
Wilberforce, Samuel, 9
World Health Organization, 13

Yeats, William Butler, 89
Yousafzai, Malala (Malala Yousafzai Malik), 26

Zepp, Ira G., 121

www.ingramcontent.com/pod-product-compliance
Lightning Source LLC
Chambersburg PA
CBHW020857160426
43192CB00007B/955